CADOGAN
gourmet guides

lazy days out
in
tuscany

*Ros Belford
Dana Facaros
and Michael Pauls*

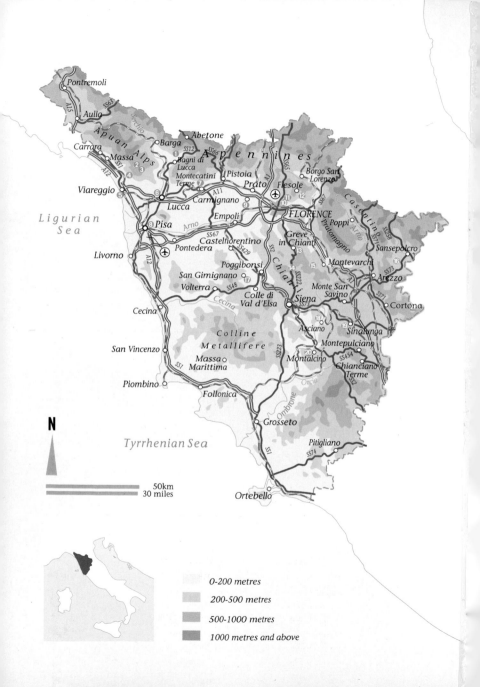

Pontremoli

Aulla

Apuan Alps

Carrara
Massa
Viareggio

Barga
Abetone
Bagni di
Lucca
Montecatini
Terme
Lucca
Pisa
Carmignano
Empoli

Apennines

Pistoia
Prato
Fiesole
Borgo San
Lorenzo

FLORENCE
Greve
in Chianti
Poppi

Casentino
Pratomagno

Sansepolcro

*Ligurian
Sea*

Livorno

Pontedera
Castelfiorentino

San Gimignano
Volterra
Poggibonsi
Colle di
Val d'Elsa

Siena

Montevarchi
Arezzo

Monte San
Savino

Cortona

Cecina

*Colline
Metallifere*

Asciano
Sinalunga

San Vincenzo

*Massa
Marittima*

Montalcino
Montepulciano
Chianciano
Terme

Piombino

Follonica

Grosseto
Pitigliano

N

Tyrrhenian Sea

50km
30 miles

Ortebello

0-200 metres

200-500 metres

500-1000 metres

1000 metres and above

CADOGAN
gourmet guides

lazy days out
in tuscany

Cadogan Books plc
London House, Parkgate Road,
London SW11 4NQ, UK

Distributed in the USA by
The Globe Pequot Press
6 Business Park Road, PO Box 833, Old Saybrook,
Connecticut 06475–0833

Copyright © Ros Belford, Dana Facaros and Michael Pauls 1996
Illustrations © Charles Shearer 1996
Book, cover and map design by Animage
Cover photography and illustration by Horacio Monteverde
Maps © Cadogan Guides, drawn by Animage and Map Creation Ltd

Series editor: Rachel Fielding
Editor: Linda McQueen

Additional editing and proof-reading
    cookery: Jane Middleton
    Italian language: Kicca Tommasi

DTP: Linda McQueen and Kicca Tommasi
Production: Rupert Wheeler Book Production Services
Printed and bound in the UK by Redwood Books Ltd , Trowbridge

ISBN 1–86011–055–X
A catalogue record for this book is available from the British Library

About the Authors

Travel writer **Ros Belford** has specialised Italy since writing the Rough Guide to Italy in 1989. She founded the Virago Women's Travel Guides, and her *Woman's Guide to Rome* was shortlisted for the Thomas Cook award in 1994. She has written books on Greece and Spain as well as Italy, and broadcasts about food and travel on Radio 4.

Thanks to... Frank Ormonde, who ate in every restaurant, read every version of every review, and told me exactly what he thought! Without his knowledge of food, and experience of running a restaurant himself, this would have been a far inferior book. He also drove over 2000km in Tuscany, put up with my many bad moods, and ate more *crostini* than most Tuscans have in a lifetime.

Meridiana (© 0171 839 2222), whose direct flights from Gatwick to Florence's extremely convenient airport made life easy (lunch is less than 20 minutes away). And to Holiday Autos (© 0171 491 1111) for providing the cars.

For recommendations and advice, to Patricia Wells of the *International Herald and Tribune*, Costanzo Martinucci of San Martino, Alvaro of La Famiglia, and Valentina Harris (whose suggestions always came up trumps and whose recipe books first turned me on to Italian cooking). And of course sincere thanks to all the restaurateurs mentioned in this book, for their hospitality, helpfulness, skills, and, of course, fine food, and for generously sharing their recipes.

Dana Facaros and Michael Pauls have written over 20 books for Cadogan. They live in a leaky old farmhouse in southwest France with their two children and assorted animals.

Please help us keep this guide up to date

Every effort has been made to ensure the accuracy of the information in this book at the time of going to press. However, standards in restaurants and practical details such as opening times and, in particular, prices are liable to change. We would be delighted to receive any comments concerning existing entries or indeed any suggestions for inclusion in future editions or companion volumes. Significant contributions will be acknowledged in the next edition, and authors of the best letters will receive a copy of the Cadogan Guide of their choice.

Contents

Introduction

Of all the regions in Italy, it is Tuscany that makes Italophiles go weakest at the knees. In virtually every town you visit there is ample evidence of its remarkable past. Perfectly preserved churches, palaces and *piazzas*; galleries stuffed with world-famous works of art; and a landscape which could still form the background for a Raphael *Madonna and Child*. And as you sit on a shady cobbled *piazza*, sipping a Campari soda and watching the locals, the way of life in Tuscany seems so civilised. It's a wealthy region, but is relatively free of the tense, workaholic culture of Lombardy, as well as of the *non mi importa niente* lethargy of the south. In Tuscany at its best you sense a balance: between work and play, reserve and exuberance, sophistication and tradition.

Tuscany was not simply the birthplace of such illustrious individuals as Leonardo, Michelangelo and Dante, but of the Renaissance itself. The Tuscany we all know is the Tuscany of the intellectuals and artists who clustered around such families as the Medici. So it might come of something of a surprise to discover that the Tuscan food most commonly found in the region's restaurants bears no traces of the region's sophisticated past, of banquets where pies of singing birds were served, or peacocks' tongues. Instead, you'll find simple, earthy peasant food, largely based around bread, tomatoes and beans.

There is a tendency in middle-class Northern Europe and the US to idealise the gastronomic traditions of peasants in southern Europe. We assume that it is impossible to eat a bad meal in Tuscany (as long as we avoid American hamburger chains) and, with critical faculties befuddled by too much sun, Chianti and Piero della Francesca, can fail to notice (or be reluctant to admit) that the food in your average Tuscan *trattoria* can be pretty boring. Such dishes as *pappa al pomodoro* (a pappy bread and tomato soup) can be wonderful if the tomatoes are sweet and ripe, the olive oil luscious, the basil freshly torn, and the chef talented. But they can be awful if the ingredients are low-quality and the chef uncaring. There is nothing in such dishes which can mask indifferent ingredients, nor a better way of proving that it is the simplest dishes which really test the ability of a chef.

To find twenty restaurants in Tuscany which we could wholeheartedly recommend, we visited over fifty. A few we could reject without staying to eat—like one establishment where there was no sign of anyone except the chain-smoking owner watching TV, or another where plates of stale *crostini* lay dismally on the bar. Others ranged from promising-looking rustic *trattorias* where we were served sauces made of unadulterated mashed up tinned tomatoes, to prize-winning temples of gastronomy where the staff treated diners as if they were

something disagreeable brought in by the cat. Sour service can curdle even the most exquisite food, while a genuine, warm welcome—whether it be the exuberant eccentricity of the three ladies at La Pievina (*see* p.120) or the disarming old-world courtesy of the waiter at Enoteca Giovanni (*see* p.38)—makes good food taste brilliant, and can leave you feeling full of the joys of humanity, even when you get caught in a post-prandial traffic jam.

Some of the most exciting restaurants in Tuscany at present are run not by trained chefs but by talented young food-lovers, who have given up careers in computing, teaching or engineering. Their families often originate from the Tuscan countryside, and some have been able to open their restaurants in the old family farm; others have had to find and finance their own premises. Wherever they are based, the restaurants they create tend to be unpretentious, tastefully—often rather minimally—decorated, and to serve food which draws its inspiration from, but is not hide-bound by, tradition. Most importantly, these new-wave restaurateurs place great importance on getting hold of the very best ingredients they can: the restaurant La Maiola (*see* p.1) scours the farms and vineyards and artisans of Tuscany and Emilia-Romagna in search of the optimum *prosciutto*, *salami* and wines, and other restaurants interested in prime quality include Trattoria Montagliari (*see* p.85); Florence's Alla Vecchia Bettola (*see* p.69) and Cibrèo (*see* p.59); and Pisa's La Mescita (*see* p.45). These are restaurants that choose to resist the ever-increasing power of the mass-produced food industry and to support artisans working in traditional ways—and, of course, most importantly of all, they know that these top-notch ingredients ensure that their food is always ahead of the crowd.

A Feast in the Mountains

Albergo Maiola

At the southern edge of the Garfagnana, the mountainous area of northern Tuscany between the Apuan Alps and the Apennines, lies the town of Bagni di Lucca, Lucca's once grand old spa, home to one of Europe's first casinos and visited by poets and writers and aristocrats since the early 1900s.

The Italians believe that the futher north in Tuscany you go, the better the cooking, graced by the kindly influences of Liguria and Emilia-Romagna. This is indeed true of Lucca and its surroundings, which have long been known for their chefs: in fact there are thousands of them all over Europe and north America. Although staples of Lucchese cuisine, such as *tordelli* (large *tortellini*), *zuppa di farro* (spelt soup) and *tacconi* (wide, flat pasta ribbons), are available all over the province, La Maiola, a restaurant in the hills above Bagni di Lucca, offers the rare opportunity to sample the sorts of foods the Lucchese would eat at festival time.

getting there

To get to La Maiola, follow the one-way system through Bagni di Lucca, keeping a sharp eye out for signs to La Maiola, the Pieve di Controne or Corsena. Once out of Bagni the road, the Via Controneria, begins an alarmingly steep climb. Keep your eyes peeled for a sign to La Maiola on the left, which directs you up a terrifyingly steep, narrow driveway through thick woods. Pray that you don't meet anyone coming in the opposite direction before you reach the restaurant.

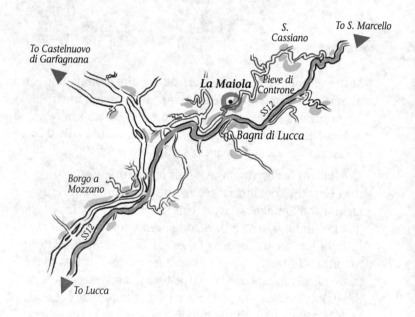

To Castelnuovo
di Garfagnana

S.
Cassiano

To S. Marcello

La Maiola

Pieve di
Controne

SS12

Bagni di Lucca

Borgo a
Mozzano

SS12

To Lucca

La Maiola

Località Maiola di Sotto, Bagni di Lucca, ℗ (0583) 86296. Closed Tues.
Booking for lunch obligatory (be sure to ask to sit outside). L25,000,
L32,000, L35,000; no credit cards.

High in the wooded hills above Bagni di Lucca is a small, unaffected and refreshingly uncommercial restaurant which serves what is probably the best food in Tuscany. It is owned by former computer engineer Enrico Franceschi and his family, and it is obvious from the moment you step through the door to a warm, gracious welcome that their restaurant is a labour of love.

The food, cooked with inspired brilliance by Enrico's wife, Simonetta, is the sort that would be served to the family on special occasions. As for the ingredients, they are so keen to serve the best possible that they even have a man with a van whose job it is to travel around Tuscany and Emilia, looking for the perfect *prosciutto* and other *salumi*. How they manage to serve the food they do at such rock-bottom prices remains a mystery. Everything is cooked to order—there are no ready-prepared sauces keeping warm— and consequently numbers are limited to 25. Service is by Enrico, his son, Francesco, and his cousin and partner, Pierluigi. All are passionately interested in food and wine, and will tell you anything you want to know about what you are eating, though they have the delicacy never to intrude.

Sit outside if you can, on the tiered, flower-filled terrace, rather than in the over-bright dining room. If you're lucky you'll get a tier to yourself. There are three set menus, one (for L32,000) concentrating on Lucchese specialities with dishes like *zuppa di farro* (spelt soup) and *coniglio con le olive* (rabbit with olives); the other is a pick-and-choose with *antipasto*, *primo*, *secondo*, *contorno*, *dolce* and a local *amaro* for a mere L25,000. For just L35,000, however, you can try the very, very best of what La Maiola has to offer. Just make sure you are hungry—though actually the food is so good that it seems to increase stomach capacity.

While you study the small, intelligent wine list, a strong, lemony aperitif and *amuse-geule* of sweet tender *pancetta* are brought to the table. If you're not sure what wine to choose, try the spicy and sophisticated red Segale from the Fattoria Luisa Roselli (in nearby San Macario al Monte), or follow the advice of Enrico, Francesco or Pierluigi.

Soon the *antipasti* start arriving. *Crostini with zucchine*, and sweet, luscious *peperonata*. Slices of crispy *polenta*, translucent golden puffs of bread dough and a fan of sweet, juicy *prosciutto*, fiery chilli-spiked *salame*, and peppery cured pork. Then a plate of baby river trout crisp in crumbs (as with whitebait, you eat the whole delectable thing).

Then come the *primi*. A surprisingly light, comforting *zuppa di farro*, made with a good strong lamb stock and eaten with generous drizzles of fruity olive oil; delicate homemade wholewheat pasta with a gutsy rabbit sauce; and springy *ravioli al ragù*. If you order in advance you can have *gnocchi* or *lasagne*.

After this there are two *secondi*: *tagliata*—basically a juicy *bistecca alla fiorentina* cut into slices around its T-bone, cooked with fresh green peppercorns; and *coniglio con le olive*—a delicius rich, pungent dish which tastes more Moroccan than Italian. Accompanying is a vegetable dish—maybe fine green beans cooked in olive oil and tomatoes.

 Find room somehow for a *dolce*—a sugar-crystallised *torta di riso*, or a moist *torta di almendra*—eaten with a light local *vin santo*, and finish up with a strong, herby locally made *digestivo*. If you can't move after lunch, there are four rooms with bathroom above the restaurant.

Coniglio con le Olive

Serves 4

1 young rabbit
1 sprig rosemary
1 clove garlic, cut in half
2 tablespoons olive oil
small glass of brandy
handful of black olives
salt and pepper

Wash the rabbit and remove all the fat. Cut into medium-sized pieces and rub each piece all over with the rosemary and garlic. Heat the olive oil in a casserole and add the pieces of rabbit. Season with salt and pepper, and cook over a high heat, turning the meat frequently, until it is golden brown all over. Pour on the brandy and let it evaporate, then add enough warm water to cover. Stir in the olives and simmer over a low heat for about an hour or until all the water has been absorbed and the rabbit is tender. Serve with roast potatoes.

---

touring around

It is a very pleasant drive up the Serchio valley from Lucca to Bagni di Lucca, so leave plenty of time to explore, either before or after lunch.

North of Lucca, the first tempting detour off SS12 is to one of the many Romanesque churches in the region, **San Giorgio di Brancoli**, near Vinchiana, as notable for its lovely setting as for its 12th-century pulpit. **Diécimo**, across the river, has a name that survives from Roman times—it lies 10 Roman miles (18km) from Lucca. The landmark here is the mighty Romanesque campanile of the 13th-century church of Santa Maria, standing out starkly against the surrounding hills. **Borgo a Mozzano**, 4km upstream, is famous for its beautiful little hogback bridge, with arches in five different shapes and sizes, dedicated to the Magdalene, or to the Devil, who according to legend built it one dark and stormy night in exchange for the first soul to cross. The clever villagers outwitted him (as they invariably do in such stories) by sending a dog over in the morning. The real builder in this case was the slightly less lethal 11th-century Countess Matilda who, besides the bridge, endowed the villages around Borgo with a set of solid Romanesque parish churches; in Borgo's church there's a wooden San Bernardino by Civitali.

To the north, just above the confluence of the Serchio river and the Torrente Lima lie the long and narrow riverside hamlets that make up the spa town of **Bagni di Lucca**, first mentioned in the days of Countess Matilda. In the early 1800s, under the patronage of Elisa Bonaparte Baciocchi, it enjoyed a moment in high society's favour—long enough to build one of Europe's first official gambling casinos (1837; roulette was invented here), an Anglican church in an exotic

Gothic Alhambra style, and an unusual 1840 suspension bridge (the Ponte alle Catene)—before sinking into obscurity. In Bagni's heyday, though, Byron, Browning, Shelley and Heine came to take the sulphur and saline waters, and perspire in a natural vapour bath. Heine was particularly enthusiastic: 'A true and proper sylvan paradise. I have never found a valley more enchanting,' he wrote; even the mountains are 'nobly formed' and not 'bizarre and Gothic like those in Germany'. Little has changed since, and these days Bagni di Lucca is a sleepy but charming little place, with some pretty villas, elegant thermal establishments that spring into action every summer, a miniature pantheon, and a fancy Circolo dei Forestieri, or foreigners' club (now a restaurant) on the river-front.

From Bagni di Lucca, the SS12 leads towards San Marcello Pistoiese and the ski resort of Abetone, following the lovely **valley of the Lima**. A byroad beginning at Bagni leads to picturesque, rugged stone hamlets like Pieve di Controne and Montefegatesi which only appear on the most detailed maps; from Montefegatesi, an unsealed road continues to the dramatic gorge of **Orrido di Botri** at the foot of the Alpe Tre Potenze (1940m). As the byroad winds back towards SS12 at Scesta, it passes **San Cassiano**, site of a fine 13th-century Pisan-style church with a delicately carved façade; in its isolated setting few people ever see it. Other byroads from the SS12 lead to tiny hamlets like Vico Pancellorum to the north and Lucchio to the south.

Family Favourites in Bandit Country

La Ceragetta

The rugged northern finger of Tuscany encompasses the region's 'Alps', the tall and jugged Alpi Apuane, which like the real Alps wear brilliant white crowns, though not made of snow—that's marble up there, the 'tears of the stars', the purest and whitest of Italy. Along the bank of the Serchio river, between the Apuan Alps and the Apennines, is the Garfagnana, a fairly undiscovered area.

The most striking thing about the Garfagnana is that it doesn't feel like Tuscany: the mountains are too steep, the forests too Alpine, the climate too extreme. What's more, of the people who do visit, the vast majority are Italians, either coming back to visit relatives, or intrepid souls wanting to explore the lesser-known parts of their country. La Ceragetta is one of the no-nonsense restaurants where Italians holidaying in the Garfagnana gather.

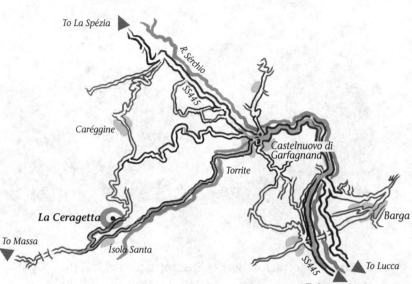

To La Spézia

R. Sérchio

SS445

Caréggine

Castelnuovo di
Garfagnana

Torrite

La Ceragetta

Barga

To Massa

Ísola Santa

To Lucca

SS445

To Lucca

getting there

From Castelnuovo di Garfagnana, take the road which heads west
to Massa and Carrara through the Apuan Alps. As soon as you have
passed Isola Santa on your left, look out for a road branching
steeply off to the right, marked with the names of various restaurants, including a red and green one for La Ceragetta. La Ceragetta
is a couple of kilometres away, a huge white chalet-style building
which looms up on your left.

La Ceragetta (di Poli Marco)

Via Ceragetta 5, Capanne di Careggine, nr Isola Santa, © (0583) 667065.
Closed Mon. L27,000, no credit cards.

You won't find anyone but Italians in this oversized Alpine chalet spectacularly located high up in the Garfagnana mountains. And though it will never win any prizes for design (artex walls), the food is simple, no-nonsense and abundant. In fact, it is not somewhere you are likely to forget in a hurry. This is the sort of restaurant where a friendly smile at the people at the next table can lead, four hours later, to a wine-flushed singalong. If you happen upon it on a quiet day, however, there are other compensations: the views from the little windows are tremendous and summer storms are real showstoppers, with black clouds scudding up the valley, accompanied by rain, lightning and thunder.

La Ceragetta is an utterly unpretentious place where scores of families pile in on holidays and at weekends and eat and drink to their hearts' content, for L27,000, all extras included. The reason prices are so cheap is that there is a single set meal every day. The meal begins with a *prosecco*, casually sloshed into a fluted glass. Then comes a bottle of basic white wine, a jug of water and a generous array of *antipasti*: borlotti beans, a chunky *panzanella* (Tuscan bread, garlic, onion and tomato salad), a delicious crispy slice of *polenta* blended with herbs and beans, and a selection of hot *crostini* topped with pungent mushrooms, a creamy chicken liver pâté, and garlicky tomatoes. There are also slices of *bresaola* and *prosciutto* and a pile of *verdure sott'aceto* (pickled vegetables).

Some time later the *primi* will begin to arrive: usually two pasta dishes and one rice. The pasta is rather unremarkable, but the wild mushroom risotto we had was delicious, creamy, flavoursome and moreish. To help your stomach prepare for the meat course, you are given a tall tubular glass of fiery *limoncello*, an intense, very yellow lemon liqueur. *Secondi* are generous—a platter of authentically chewy grilled rabbit, veal and beef—served with a mixed leaf salad.

There's a range of desserts, including (wait for it) local *pecorino* with local honey dribbled over it. The guy who sang 'Volare' assured us the contrast of tangy salt and sweet honey was great.

Infarinata

Serves 4–6

The polenta served at La Ceragetta is typical of the Garfagnana.

1.2 litres/2 pints water
2 teaspoons salt
300g/11oz coarse-grained cornmeal (polenta)
450g/1lb mixed vegetables (e.g. diced carrot, celery or
onions, any green leafy vegetables like spinach,
kohlrabi or chard, cooked borlotti or flageolet beans)
extra virgin olive oil

Bring the water and salt to the boil in a large heavy-based saucepan. Add the cornmeal in a thin, steady stream, stirring all the time to prevent any lumps forming. Add the vegetables and cook gently for around 40 minutes, stirring constantly. The polenta is ready when it is stiff enough to be pulled away easily from the sides of the pan. Pour the polenta into a damp glass bowl and smooth the surface with a wet knife. Cover and let it rest for at least 10 minutes, then turn out on to a board. Cut the polenta into slices about 1cm/½ inch thick, arrange on a serving plate and drizzle with olive oil.

Alternatively you can deep-fry the slices of polenta until crisp and golden.

---

touring around

Ten kilometres east of La Ceragetta, in the heart of the Garfagnana, is the lively little town of **Castelnuovo di Garfagnana**, the region's 'capital', guarded by the Rocca, a fine castle decorated in the best 14th-century manner. Its most famous commander was poet Ludovico Ariosto, author of that great Renaissance epic poem of chivalry and fantasy, *Orlando Furioso*. Ariosto, in the employ of the Este Dukes of Ferrara, competently chased bandits and collected tolls here from 1522–5, but didn't enjoy the job. 'I'm not a man to govern other men,' he wrote to his lover in Ferrara. 'I have too much pity, and can't deny the things they require me to deny.'

Castelnuovo makes an excellent base for excursions into its often wild surroundings. To the northeast, past the small resort of Castiglione di Garfagnana, a tortuous mountain road continues through 16km of magnificent scenery to the **Foce delle Radici** (the pass into Emilia-Romagna) and **San Pellegrino in Alpe**, with magnificent views and an ancient monastery, and a good little ethnographic museum, the Museo della Campagna (*open 9.30–1 and 3–7 July–Sept; at other times ✆ 649 072*). West of Castelnuovo a truly scenic road leads over the Apuan Alps to Carrara and the coast, through the desolate valley of the Turrite Secca, its sombre features relieved by the romantic little oasis of **Isola Santa**—a tiny village in the trees on its own tiny lake, once a hideout for medieval renegades; now it is abandoned, save for a few old folks and the sheep who live behind the altar of the church. The first turning on the right after Isola Santa climbs up into the hills, passing the Ceragetta restaurant.

Continuing beyond the restaurant you'll come to **Careggine**, a lofty old hamlet with commanding views, and the artificial **Lago di Vagli**. Creating this lake submerged the medieval village of Fabbriche, of

Castello Malaspina

which the top of the campanile may still be seen sticking stubbornly out of the water. Carrying on along the same road, you rejoin the main valley road at Poggio. From here there is a choice: you can either head north into the **Lunigiana**, or back into the mountains to the stunning village of **Vagli Sopra**, village of old marble quarries and an 18th-century road, now deteriorated into a footpath, which leads into the comely **Valle di Arnetola**. Towering over all is **Monte Pisanino** (1945m), the tallest of the Apuan Alps; the road approaching the summit and the alpine refuge of Donegani, by way of the lakelet of Gramolazzo, begins at Piazza al Serchio, where you leave both the Serchio and the Garfagnana behind.

Alternatively, beyond Piazza al Serchio, the first town of consequence along the SS445 is fortified **Casola in Lunigiana** (20km); just beyond it a road veers south for the tiny spa of **Equi Terme** in the mountains above. Equi is less visited these days for its waters than for its cave, charmingly called La Buca del Cane (Dog's Hole) after its relics of pre-historic man's best friend (*open 9–12 and 2–5, summer 9–12 and 4–7; adm*). Our ancestors also apparently socialized with bears (or ate them), judging by the bones found here. **Fivizzano** to the north (on SS63 or by road from Casola) belonged to the Malaspina of Massa until the Medici snatched it and fortified it as a grand ducal outpost. The main square, Piazza Medicea, has a grand fountain paid for by Cosimo III, a few Florentine-style palaces, and the 13th-century parish church. There are two interesting Romanesque chapels in the vicinity, **Santa Maria Assunta**, 3km towards Pognana, in a lovely isolated setting, and 12th-century **San Paolo a Vendaso** with carved capitals inside, on SS63 towards the Passo di Cerreto. From Ceserano, just south of SS445, SS446 heads southwest over the mountains to Sarzana, passing by way of **Fosdinovo**, the Malaspina castle that hosted Dante in 1306, one of the most beautiful and majestic in the Lunigiana. Inside there's an interesting collection of arms and ornaments found in tombs (*open daily 10–12, 4–7, 3–7 weekends, in winter 9–12, 3–6; adm*).

A Trout Stream in the Garfagnana

For many years the chief export of the Garfagnana region of northern Tuscany has been Italians; the green hills and mountains, the narrow valley of the Serchio between the Apennines and the Apuan Alps, the stone villages perched on slopes that look so picturesque on postcards were simply never generous enough to provide a sufficient livelihood for their inhabitants. Even today, villages like Fornovolasco, where

Grotta del Vento

you'll be having lunch, are semi-abandoned, springing to life for a few weeks in August, when the younger generations who have left the Garfagnana for a more comfortable life in the city return to visit relatives.

The chief staple of the district until recently was flour made from chestnuts, and chestnut groves still cover much of the region. Indeed, if you're visiting in October, you should be able to collect a good supply for yourself. Dishes—both sweet and savoury—are made from chestnuts and their flour: one delicious Garfagnana speciality is *necci*, thin chestnut flour pancakes, eaten as they are cooked, wrapped around a dollop of *ricotta* and good fruit jam. Other local foods to look out for on menus are wild mushrooms and river trout.

getting there

From Barga follow the spectacular mountain road to Fornovolasco. Cross the stream and turn sharp right into the village's only parking space. The Rifugio La Buca is the white chalet-style building right next to the stream.

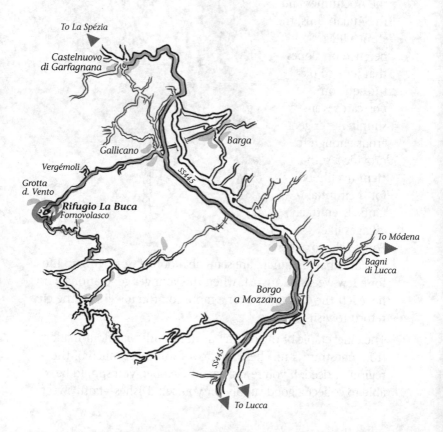

Rifugio La Buca

Fornovolasco, ℗ (0583) 722013. Closed Fri from Nov to Easter. L35,000, no credit cards.

With its fake Alpine chalet make-over and plastic bead curtains, this looks like the sort of restaurant to avoid at all cost, even if it does stand by a fast-flowing stream at the heart of an appealingly decaying hamlet surrounded by dense woodland and staggering mountains. In fact, La Buca's apparent naffness has probably been its saviour. Most middle-class tourists heading up to the Grotta del Vento would take one look at the place—and the posse of old men sucking on sour cigarettes outside the adjoining bar—and opt for a picnic.

La Buca is no gastronomic temple, but it does have a great atmosphere, good honest food, and an effortlessly gluggable house white for L3000 a bottle—the price of duty paid on a single bottle in the UK. What's more, if you pass through those bead curtains in high summer you'll walk straight into a party. Grandfathers, grandmothers, aunties, uncles, cousins, in-laws, teenagers and new-born babies pack huge tables, chattering and gurgling away as the mums dole out oodles of quivering tagliatelle and heaps of golden *tortelli* from vast oval platters.

Service, by efficient women in overalls, is brisk, no-nonsense and matter of fact: within seconds of ordering, an ice-cold bottle of refreshing country white will arrive. Following close on its heels there'll be a basket of fresh, coarse rustic bread. The *antipasto*—basic *crostini* (one of them topped with a substance with a suspicious resemblance to sandwich spread) is best avoided. Save room instead for a pile of lubricious *tagliatelle ai funghi*, generously laced with flavoursome wild mushrooms and olive oil. Alternatively you can have the mushrooms with *cannelloni*, *tortelli*, or *spaghetti*, or any of the pastas with tomatoes, *ragù* or *all'arrabbiata*.

Best of the *secondi* is the excellent tasty grilled river trout. Although it comes from a farm downstream it is authentic brown trout, not the rainbow trout you get in England. The difference is huge. Otherwise you could opt for a vast (and amazingly cheap) *bistecca*. The mixed leaf salad is fresh and crispy and the olive oil fruity. Puddings vary according to season—if you're lucky there will be miniature wild strawberries (the sort which cost £7.50 a pound in Harrods) and blackcurrents—ask to have them neat, without the synthetic ice cream.

Trota alle Erbe

Tuscany, and in particular the Garfagnana's, many fast-flowing streams mean that there is plenty of good quality brown trout around. This recipe is used all over Tuscany.

Serves 4

4 river trout, cleaned
2 tablespoons red wine vinegar
small bunch flat-leaf parsley, finely chopped
1 clove garlic, finely chopped
5 shallots, finely chopped
1 tablespoon lemon juice
3–4 tablespoons extra virgin olive oil
a few basil leaves, to garnish
salt and pepper

For the poaching liquid:
2 litres/3 ½ pints water
1 glass dry white wine
1 tablespoon lemon juice
handful of parsley leaves
a few basil leaves
1 large clove garlic, chopped
2 shallots, chopped

Put the trout in a bowl, pour over water to cover and add the vinegar. Leave to soak while you prepare the poaching liquid. Put all the ingredients in a large pan, bring to the boil and simmer for 35 minutes. Strain the broth and pour it into a fish kettle.

The broth needs to cool for 30 minutes, so while you are waiting prepare the sauce. Put the parsley, garlic and shallots in a glass bowl, stir in the lemon juice and olive oil, and mix well. Season to taste.

Drain the trout and pat them dry with paper towels. Place the trout in the fish kettle, bring just to a simmer over a medium heat and poach for 5 minutes or so. Drain the trout and arrange on a serving dish. Give the sauce a good stir, pour it over the trout, and sprinkle with torn basil leaves.

touring around

The Garfagnana proper begins south of Barga where the Lima flows into the river Serchio at Fornoli. In the 14th century this area was ruled by the kinsmen of Castruccio Castracani; one of their prettiest mountain hamlets is **Tereglio**, along the scenic northeast road to the Alpe Tre Potenze, before it meanders on to Abetone. The Castracani had their base up at **Coreglia Antelminelli**, high above the Serchio and the main SS445 (turn off at Piano di Coreglia). Coreglia's parish church contains a magnificent 15th-century processional cross, and there's a Museo della Figurina devoted to the Garfagnana's traditional manufacture of plaster figures (*open summer 8–1 during the week and 10–1, 4–7 weekends; winter 8–1, closed Sun; adm*).

To the north, the lovely hill town of **Barga** (pop. 11,000) stands above its modern offspring, Fornaci di Barga, on the main SS445. Barga was astute enough to maintain its independence until 1341, when it decided to link its fortunes with Florence. At the very top of town stands Barga's chief monument, its cathedral, begun in the year 1000 on a terrace, with a panoramic view over the rooftops and of surrounding hills apparently clad in green velvet, and bare mountains scoured with white marble. Built of a blonde stone called *alberese di Barga*, its square façade is discreetly decorated with a shallow pattern, charming reliefs and two leering lions; on the side the *campanile* is incorporated into the church; over the portal, there's a relief of a feast scene with a king and dwarfs. There's yet another dwarf inside, supporting one of the red marble pillars of the pulpit by the idiosyncratic 13th-century Como sculptor, Guido Bigarelli. The other pillars required a pair of lions, one grinning over a conquered dragon, one being both stroked and stabbed by a man. Less mysterious are the naive reliefs around the pulpit itself, startlingly sophisticated versions of familiar scriptural scenes. In the choir note the venerable polychrome wood statue of St Christopher (early 1100s) and a choir screen with more strange medieval carvings, including a mystic mermaid. Around the back, the cathedral's garden has a magnificent Lebanon cedar. Next to the cathedral stands the Palazzo Pretorio and 14th-century Loggetta del Podestà; if you go down the stairs towards the dungeon you can see Barga's old corn measures—a medieval Bureau of Standards.

The rest of Barga is a photogenic ensemble of archways and little *palazzi* piled on top of each other, with walls, gates and a ravine planted with kitchen gardens. Things get lively in July and August with the classes and performances of Opera Barga in the old Teatro Dei Differenti, founded in 1600. Between Barga and Fornaci di Barga, you can measure the showy success of the city's emigrants who returned to build modern palaces in the suburb of Giardino.

After lunch at La Buca, potholers and non-claustrophobes should make a point of visiting Fornovalasco's main attraction, Tuscany's best cave, the **Grotta del Vento** (*open April–Sept, at other times Sun and holidays only. Guided tours of one or two hours; 10–12 and 2–6; at 10 and 2, 3-hour tours for real cave fiends; adm exp try to come in the morning when it's less crowded; for information, © (0583) 722 024 ☎ 722 053*). It's a long cavern of fat stalactites, bottomless pits and abysses, and subterranean lakes and streams, set in a barren, eerie landscape.

Fish in an Olive Mill

The Etruscan Riviera, the Tyrrhenian shore, Tuscany by the sea—call it what you will, most of it is flat, straight and endowed with wide sandy beaches that are usually crowded; it is hard to escape the Italian beach culture of privately owned shoreline densely packed with deckchairs and beach umbrellas. Viareggio is just one of many resorts along the coast, originally little more than a fishing village, but by the turn of the century a booming seaside resort with a celebrated promenade.

The coast is backed by the Apuan Alps and by towns such as Carrara, famous for its snow-white marble, and Pietrasanta, a mellow old town also rich in marbly traditions. For the best place to eat in Viareggio, *see* p.25; however, if you want to eat excellent, inspiringly cooked fish without all the coastline razzamatazz, head for La Martinatica, an ancient *frantoio* or olive mill just outside Pietrasanta, which has been converted into a restaurant by mother and son team, Mirella and Riccardo Pardini.

Trattoria La Martinatica

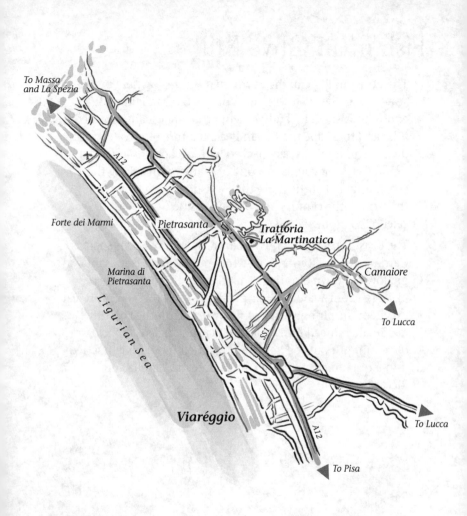

getting there

From Pietrasanta follow the signs to Camaiore, passing a cemetery
(invisible behind high walls) on your right, and a Fina garage and
then an Audi garage on your left. La Martinatica is signposted to
the left up a narrrow track just after the Audi garage.

Trattoria La Martinatica

Località Baccatoio, Via Martinatica 20, Pietrasanta, © (0584) 792534.
Closed Wed, hols, November. L55,000–65,000, all credit cards.

The old mill which houses the *trattoria* straddles a fast-running stream; you can see the water wheel which once operated the olive press as you walk inside, and you can eat outside on a wooden platform which protrudes over the water—wonderfully cool and refreshing in summer.

Inside, the kitchen opens on to the dining room, heftily beamed, slightly damp and covered in pink wallpaper. Baskets of good fresh crusty bread and cubes of moist salt-crusted *focaccia* sit ready on the tables, which is just as well as it gives you something to do while you wait for the rather slow waitress.

There's are two daily menus, one meat and one fish (served on alternate days), but you can have just a few dishes if you want.

It's the fish you should really come for—it's better here than at Gambero Rosso in San Vincenzo, widely touted as the best restaurant in Italy. There's a large wine list, but you won't go far wrong it you opt for the characterful (and great value) Montellori Sauvignon. *Antipasti* tend to be light and delicate, like *pescespada affumicato*, a for once not too salty smoked swordfish served with shavings of fennel and a generous drizzle of fine olive oil; and *paté di trota*, a subtle trout pâté with a thin crust of nuts, dotted with whole black peppercorns.

There will probably be a longish pause for the *primi*—but an hour would not be too long to wait for Riccardo's *ravioli al nasello*, with the virtually translucent pasta rippling over a tasty, textured hake filling, or the *spaghetti al nero con gamberetti*, a glistening tangle of squid-ink-black spaghetti spiked with shavings of chilli and garlic topped with a juicy mound of utterly fresh prawns. The *secondi* are always wonderful: Riccardo and Mirella are chefs who know when to let well alone, so your fish is not going to be overwhelmed with a fancy sauce. If you're really lucky, there might be lobster—simply boiled and served with a pile of cannellini beans (a great combination). Or a pile of mussels and clams, served,

Tuscan style, with its garlic, wine, tomato and chilli broth over a slice of country bread.

Desserts are no let-down. Look out for the refreshing *budino di ricotta e limone con salsa di fragola*, a ricotta and lemon mould with a simple strawberry coulis, or a fittingly decadent chocolate mousse. Coffee is probably a necessity, but you can relax before heading off in the little garden.

Cozze e Vongole Stufate in Guazzetto

Serves 6

675g/1½lb mussels
675g/1½lb clams
1 lemon
2 tablespoons extra virgin olive oil
1 medium carrot, finely chopped
1 medium red onion, finely chopped
1 large clove garlic, finely chopped
a good handful of flat-leaf parsley, chopped
2 bay leaves
a large pinch dried chilli flakes
1 large glass (225ml/8fl oz) dry white wine
6 large slices crusty Tuscan bread
salt and pepper

Wash the clams and mussels, de-bearding the mussels. Place in a bowl of cold water with the juice from the lemon and the squeezed-out lemon halves. Leave for 30 minutes.

Heat the oil in a casserole, add the carrot, garlic and parsley and sweat for ten minutes. Add the bay leaves and season with salt, pepper and chilli flakes. Stir in the wine and boil until reduced by half. Rinse and drain the mussels and clams and add to the casserole. Cover and cook for 4–5 minutes or until the shells open. Season to taste, and remove the bay leaves and any mussels and clams that remain closed.

Transfer the shellfish to a serving platter with a slotted spoon and keep warm. Boil the sauce for about a minute, stirring constantly until slightly reduced.

Toast the bread, and place a slice on each serving plate. Pour some of the sauce over the toast and let each person help themselves to clams, mussels and more sauce.

touring around

An ideal day out would be to explore **Pietrasanta** in the morning, then after lunch drive up into the mountains beyond. Pietrasanta's walls date from 1255, though its regular quadrangle of streets suggests a Roman origin. Life centres around the large central Piazza del Duomo, with its Florentine Marzocco on a pillar (1514) and the Duomo di San Martino, begun in 1256 and restored in 1630 and 1824, with a rose window carved from a single block of marble and more marble inside, as well as a bronze crucifix by Tacca and a 13th-century fresco by the school of Giotto. Its Renaissance campanile looks half-finished. It shares the piazza with the Palazzo Pretorio and Sant'Agostino (14th century) with an attractive minimalist Pisan façade. From here a road leads up to the citadel, or Rocca Arrighina, built in the 1300s by Castruccio Castracani and lit up at night; it often hosted emperors on their way to Rome but all they left behind is the view. You can see what contemporary would-be Michelangelos are up to by calling Cosmave, ✆ (0585) 791 297, ✇ 790 885, who will give information about the work of local artists. Alternatively turn right from the main gate for the central market building, its parking adorned with the world's most erotic market statue, of a woman *en déshabille* pulling a young bull after her.

From Pietrasanta a road heads inland towards **Valdicastello Carducci** (birthplace of the poet Giosuè Carducci), passing by way of the 9th-century Pieve dei Santi Giovanni e Felicita, the oldest church in the Versilia, with 14th-century frescoes. There are lovely views stretching from La Spezia to Pisa from Capezzano and Capriglia, on the same road winding further up in the mountains. **Camaiore** (from the Roman Campus Major, pop. 31,000) is an industrial town on the road

Facciata della pieve dei Santi Giovanni Battista e Stefano

to Lucca, of interest for its Romanesque churches—the Collegiata, Santi Giovanni Battista Stefano (with a stately bell tower and Roman sarcophagus for a font), and the 8th-century Badia dei Santi Benedettini, remodelled in the 11th century and adorned with a lovely portal. In Piazza Diaz, the little Museo d'Arte Sacra contains some lovely Flemish tapestries (*open 10–12 Sat only, summer 4–6 Tues and Sat*). A panoramic road from Camaiore leads up to **Monteggiori**, with more fine views. Other destinations around Camaiore include the beautiful **Valle Freddana** and **Monte Magno**, and **Pieve a Elici**, near Massarosa, with another excellent Romanesque church, 12th-century San Pantaleone. From here a minor road continues up through majestic chestnut groves to **Montigiano**, one of the finest balconies in the Apuans.

Puccini, Fish and Fun

Viareggio, on the Tuscan coast just north of Pisa, is a big, brash seaside resort with some great Art Nouveau buildings. With its Shrove Tuesday carnival and Puccini opera festival, its neat grid of interlocking streets and its celebrated promenade, it is well worth seeing, even if it is not somewhere you'd want to linger, as a flamboyant monument to *fin de siècle* fun.

Anyway, after lunch in the delightfully unassuming Giorgio, where the fish is so fresh that it practically jumps by itself in the pan, you can head off to the beautiful Lake Massaciuccoli where Puccini would retreat from the glittering world of grand opera and spend his days shooting ducks.

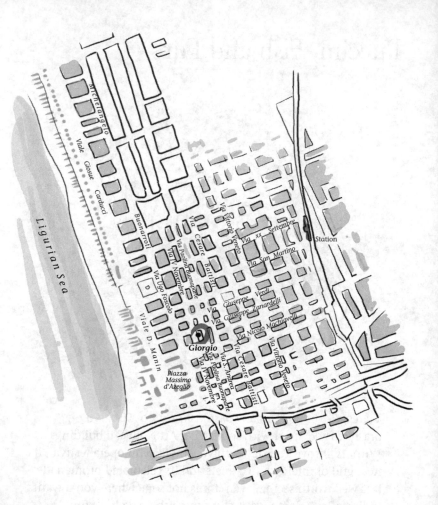

getting there

Once in Viareggio, follow signs for the centre, which should bring you to the seafront. Park in Piazza Massimo d'Azeglio, the first car park you come to after the port, then walk up a block to Via IV Novembre. Turn left and walk on for a few blocks until you reach Via Zanardelli. The restaurant is on the corner of the two streets.

Giorgio

Via Zanardelli (corner with Via IV Novembre), Viareggio, © (0584) 44493.
Closed Wed. L45,000 excluding wine, all credit cards.

Giorgio's may be just a couple of blocks from Viareggio's sea-front, but it's a world away from the resort's cheap glamour and razzamatazz. What's more, you can eat here for half the price you would on the promenade. This quaint old-fashioned fish restaurant, founded some time in the Sixties, has artex walls, collections of football banners, copper pans and fish posters; an assembly of amateurish paintings (lots of doe-eyed Seventies girls with improbably long false eyelashes); and solemn waiters who look as though they have never seen the sun. There is, however, always one thing about Giorgio's which is uncompromisingly up-to-date—immediately inside the entrance are trays of sharp-eyed and glistening fish and seafood lying on beds of ice, scampi, clams, sole, red mullet (*triglia*), bream (*orata*), sea bass (*branzino*) and turbot (*rombo*).

The wine list is limited: there are three house whites (a fresh Montecarlo, Pinot Grigio and a local *frizzante*) while more superior wines include Gavi di Gavi, a Villa Banfi Pinot Grigio, a white from Castello di Ama and a tocai from Friuli.

If you like tasting a little bit of all sorts, start with the *misto mare caldo*, a delicious selection of tender, meaty octopus, a salad of crayfish tails, prawns, rocket and orange, herby fish croquettes, and stuffed tomatoes. If this doesn't appeal, look out for an *insalata di polpo e gamberi* (octopus and prawn salad), or a warm *carpaccio* of sea-bass. To follow there are some tasty pasta dishes: *spaghetti alla trabaccolara*—*spaghetti* laced with a flavoursome sauce of tomato, olive oil and scorpion fish—and *tagliolini alla Giorgio*, a subtle mixture of *scampi*, ricotta and lemon. There's also a hearty *spaghetti alle vongole veraci*, and a good fish soup, *minestra di pesce*.

The range of *secondi* is huge: *fritto misto* (a mixture of deep-fried fish), *triglie alla livornese* (red mullet cooked with tomato), oven-baked gilt-head or sea bass, grilled red mullet, steamed turbot, turbot with olives, grilled scampi or grilled lobster...really, though, with fish this fresh you should go for one cooked as simply as possible—the baked sea bass, the steamed turbot and the grilled red mullet are all delicious. All you need to accompany is a good green salad.

Although desserts do not feature strongly, there is a superb lemon ice cream, a deft creamy, tangy, bitter-sweet combination that works as a great *digestivo*.

Triglie alla Livornese

Serves 6

3 tablespoons extra virgin olive oil
3 garlic cloves, chopped
600g/1lb 5oz plum tomatoes, peeled and puréed
6 large red mullet, cleaned
seasoned flour for dusting
olive oil for deep frying
2 tablespoons chopped flat-leaf parsley
salt and pepper

In a heavy saucepan heat the extra virgin olive oil and fry the garlic gently until translucent. Stir in the tomatoes and cook for about 15 minutes until the sauce is fairly thick. Season to taste.

Wash the fish and pat dry, then dust with seasoned flour. Heat the oil for deep-frying in a large heavy pan and fry the fish one at a time until golden and cooked through. Drain the fish on kitchen paper, then place in the sauce and heat for a few minutes. Adjust the seasoning and serve sprinkled with the chopped parsley.

touring around

Viareggio is now Tuscany's biggest seaside resort, but up until the 1820s it was little more than a fishing village, named after the medieval royal road, the 'Via Regia', that connected Migliarino and Pietrasanta. After the 14th-century battles with Pisa, Genoa and Florence, this little village was the republic of Lucca's sole access to the sea. Fortifications were built—Forte del Motrone (which it lost in

1441) and the Torre del Mare and Torre Matilde near the canal (open on request), which the Lucchesi managed to hold on to until the 19th century. It was Lucca's beloved Duchess Maria Luisa who drained the swamps, developed the shipyards and fishing and resort industries, and laid out the neat grid of streets; by the 1860s the first *cabanas* and beach umbrellas had made their début.

By the turn of the century Viareggio was booming, embellished with playful, intricate wooden Art Nouveau buildings that lined its celebrated seaside promenade, the **Passeggiata Viale Regina Margherita**. In 1917 a massive fire destroyed nearly all of this, and when it was rebuilt in the 1920s its most important buildings were designed by Galileo Chini and the eclectic Alfredo Belluomini. Chini (1873–1956) was one of the founders of Italian Art Nouveau, or the Liberty Style, which first caught the public's fancy in the 1902 Esposizione Internazionale di Arti Decorative in Turin. Chini was especially well known for florid ceramics, but he also designed stage sets for the New York Metropolitan Opera's premières of his friend Puccini's opera: *Turandot*, *Manon Lescaut* and *Gianni Scicchi*, as well as the throne room of the King of Siam (1911–14). In Viareggio he worked with Belluomini to produce what has become the symbol of Viareggio, the colourful, twin-towered **Gran Caffè Margherita**, in a kind of Liberty-Mannerism; as well as the Bagna Balena and what is now the Supercinema, all on the Passeggiata. You can compare their work with the 1900 Negozio Martini, the only wooden building to survive the 1917 fire. Chini and Belluomini also designed a number of hotels as well as Puccini's villa on Piazza Puccini, and the buildings at Piazza D'Azeglio 15 and Viale Manin 20.

Even more colourful are the floats used in Viareggio's famous **Carnival**. It was begun in the 1890s but has grown to rival the much older carnivals of Rome and Venice, and in pure frivolity has surpassed them all. In the centre of the action are large, usually very satirical papier-mâché floats; if you can't come on Shrove Tuesday to join the massive parade, you can see them being created in the huge float hangars along Viale Marco Polo and they are displayed in the **Hangar Carnivale** (*open 10.30–12, 4.30–7 Tues–Fri*). At the **Società Ippica Viareggina**, Via Comparini 8, © 391176, you can hire a horse to explore the pine woods that lie just south of Viareggio.

puccini's piano

After lunch at Giorgio, you can set off for a quieter afternoon in search of Puccini. The maestro from Lucca spent most of his later years in his villa at Torre del Lago, 6km south of Viareggio along Via dei Tigli (buses from Piazza D'Azeglio), a lovely road passing through an extensive pine wood. His villa, now the **Museo Pucciniano** (*open 10–12.30 and 3–5, 4–7 daily in summer, closed Mon; adm*), is on the banks of shallow Lake Massaciuccoli, where he could practise 'my second favourite instrument, my rifle' on passing coots. The villa contains its original furnishings, old photos, the piano on which Puccini composed many of his operas, his rifles and other mementoes. The maestro and his wife and son are buried in the adjacent chapel. In August Torre del Lago holds a popular opera festival in its outdoor theatre, presenting famous and obscure works by the great composer; for a schedule and tickets contact the Festival Pucciniano, Piazzale Belvedere Puccini, Torre del Lago, © (0584) 359322.

Most of Lake Massaciuccoli and the marshlands, the macchia, and beaches to the south are part of the **Parco Naturale Migliarino San Rossore Massaciuccoli** (*guided tours are arranged from 8am to 2pm, phone in advance, © (050) 525 500*). Boats from Torre del Lago explore some of these wetlands, or you can go by car to the tiny village of **Massaciuccoli**. The wild beaches between Viareggio and Torre del Lago, with their low dunes and scrubby pine forest, are free and undeveloped. The forest of **San Rossore**, in existence since Roman times, is nowadays threatened by the spray from the polluted sea, which is unfortunately killing the pines (*San Rossore is open Sundays and holidays only, 8.30–5.30 winter, till 7.30 summer; to visit on weekdays call © (050) 539111*).

La Buca a Lucca

Ask most Toscanophiles which town they'd most like to live
in, and the likelihood is that they'll say Lucca. Of all Tuscany's
great cities, Lucca is the most cosy, sane and domestic, a tidy
traffic-free gem of a town encased within the best preserved
walls in Italy. Even these seem more like garden walls than
something that would keep enemies at bay. The old ramparts
and surrounding areas, once the outworks of the fortifications,
are now full of lawns and trees, forming a miniature green
belt; on the walls, where the little city's soldiers once
patrolled, citizens ride their bicycles and walk their dogs. La
Buca di Sant'Antonio, just off Piazza San Michele, is likewise
sane and civilized, founded in 1887 and still redolent of
bygone days.

Gastronomically, Lucca is probably best known for its luscious
fruity olive oil, reckoned to be the finest in Tuscany, a drizzle
of which can make an average soup into an unforgettable
experience. But there's more to Lucca than olive oil, for the
town stands between the sea and the mountains, and has a

La Buca di Sant'Antonio

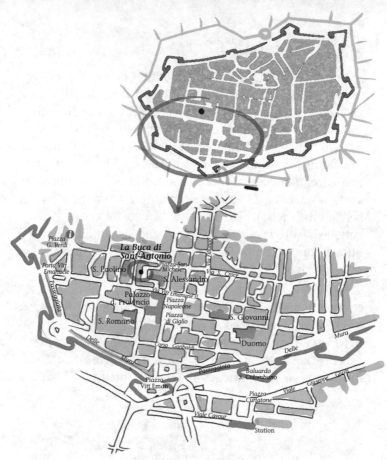

particularly varied cusine: sea and freshwater fish, wild mushrooms, chestnuts, *farro* (spelt), pork, lamb, poultry and game. Also, as you are wandering the town, look out for *buccellato*, an ring-shaped aniseed-flavoured cake best eaten in summer with strawberries.

getting there

There are no cars allowed within Lucca's walls, so park at the railway station, which stands outside one of the main pedestrian entrances to the town. Walk round the Duomo, past San Giovanni, across Piazza di Giglio and Piazza Napoleone and right up Via Veneto. This brings you up to the main market square, Piazza San Michele. The restaurant is just off the square, to your left.

La Buca di Sant'Antonio

Via della Cervia 1, Lucca, © (0583) 55881. Closed Sun eve and Mon, hols, three weeks in July. L50,000, all major credit cards.

La Buca di Sant'Antonio is a rather august, old-fashioned place, founded in 1887 and decorated with what appear to be the instruments of an entire brass band. It has the air of a pre-war provincial restaurant, with everything running as smoothly and comfortably as a favourite old pocket watch. Most of the waiters have been here for years, and glide around the restaurant, serving with a friendly, unobtrusive grace. Their ease is infectious, and there's a lovely relaxed hum to the place at lunchtime, with local businessmen, families and the occasional couple of tourists, all made to feel equally at home. Food tends towards the traditional, with dishes like *coppa di Zibello* (cured neck of pork from a local village), *ravioli di ricotta alle zucchine* (ricotta-stuffed ravioli with courgettes) and *capretto nostrale*, Garfagnana kid cooked on the spit with sage-roast potatoes. But there are plenty of other dishes worth trying.

Although the wine list is heavily weighted towards Tuscany, there are wines from other regions as well. However, the cheapest local white, a Colli Lucchese from the Fattoria Fondin il Camilioni, is an excellent lunchtime wine—young, refreshing and slightly *pétillant*.

Fish is best eaten as an *antipasto* rather than a *secondo*. The *carpaccio di trota salmonata* is gorgeous, the slivers of salmon trout juicily marinated in lemon and served with a mixed salad. *Alici fresche* (fresh anchovies) are also worth trying, succulent and totally unsalty.

As for *primi*, at least one of the table should try *bavette al pesto*, the *bavette* (a sort of flat spaghetti) perfectly *al dente* and topped with a dollop of delicate, fragrant pesto. If you want cheese, the waiter will bring a huge wedge of grainy *pecorino stagionato* to grate over it. Other good choices are local dishes like the robust *zuppa di farro* and the comforting *ravioli di ricotta con zucchine* or the *tordelli lucchesi* which are a bit like giant *tortelloni*, stuffed with a tasty filling of meat, chard and *ricotta* and served with a meat sauce.

 For *secondo* opt for something local like the spit-roast kid, *agnello in umido con olive nere*, or *fritto di costolette d'agnello con carciofi* (a mouthwatering combination of fried lamb and artichoke). In season, mushroom addicts should go for *funghi porcini al cartoccio*—a gargantuan portion of meaty *porcini* cooked in a paper bag. As a side dish order *fagioli nostrali all'olio*, a perfectly cooked dish of white beans over which you should drizzle abundant quantities of the fruity local olive oil—there are several oils to choose from in the restaurant.

Finally, don't leave without trying the *torta di castagne* if it is on the menu—a flan filled with a delectably sticky, delicate chestnut cream.

Agnello in Umido con Olive Nere

Serves 4

5 tablespoons olive oil, preferably from Lucca
2 cloves garlic, finely chopped
½ onion, finely chopped
1 sprig rosemary, finely chopped
1kg/2¼lb leg or shoulder of young lamb, cut into 5cm/2 inch chunks
1 glass white wine
4 tablespoons tomato purée
500ml/18fl oz meat stock
200g/7oz bitter olives
salt and pepper

Heat the olive oil in a casserole, add garlic, onion and rosemary and cook gently until soft. Add the lamb and brown all over. Raise the heat, add the wine, and let it evaporate while stirring in the tomato purée, salt and pepper. Pour in the stock, cover and cook over a low heat for 50–60 minutes or until the lamb is tender, adding the olives about 15 minutes before the end of the cooking time.

touring around

Lucca's rigid grid of streets betrays its Roman origins; it was founded as a colony in 180 BC as *Luca*, and in 56 BC entered the annals of history when Caesar, Pompey and Crassus met here to form the ill-fated First Triumvirate. It was converted to Christianity early on by St Peter's disciple Paulinus, who became first bishop of Lucca. The city did especially well in the Dark Ages; in late Roman times it was the administrative capital of Tuscany, and under the Goths managed to repulse the murderous Lombards; its extensive archives were begun in the 8th century, and many of its churches were founded shortly after. By the 11th and 12th centuries Lucca emerged as one of the leading trading towns of Tuscany, specializing in the production of silk, sold by colonies of merchants in the East and West, who earned enough to make sizeable loans to Mediterranean potentates. A Lucchese school of painting developed, such as it is, and beautiful Romanesque churches were erected, influenced by nearby Pisa.

Like paradise, Lucca is entered by way of St Peter's Gate. Immediately inside you'll find the splendidly ornate apse of **St Martin's Cathedral**, perhaps the most outstanding work of the Pisan style outside Pisa, begun in the 11th century and completed only in the 15th. Stacked above the assymmetrical arcaded porch are three levels of colonnades, with pillars arranged like candy sticks, while behind and on the arches are exquisite 12th- and 13th-century reliefs and sculpture—the best work Lucca has to offer.

The dark interior offers an excellent introduction to the works of Lucca's one and only great artist, sculptor Matteo Civitali (1435–1501). His most famous work is the octagonal **Tempietto** (1484), a marble tabernacle in the middle of the left aisle, containing Lucca's most precious holy relic, the *Volto Santo* ('Holy Image'), a cedar-wood crucifix said to be a true portrait of Jesus, sculpted by Nicodemus, an eyewitness to the crucifixion. Long an object of pilgrimage, the image goes out for a night on the town in a candlelight procession every 13 September.

Further up the left aisle a chapel contains Fra Bartolomeo's *Virgin and Child Enthroned*, and, in the transept, the remarkable **Tomb of Ilaria**

del Carretto (1408), perhaps Jacopo della Quercia's most beautiful work. Here, too, is an altar by Giambologna. Civitali carved the cathedral's high altar, and also two expressive tombs in the south transept. A door from the right aisle leads to the sacristy, with a good *Madonna Enthroned with Saints* by Domenico Ghirlandaio; a side altar near here has a typically strange composition from Tintoretto, a *Last Supper* with a nursing mother in the foreground and cherubs floating around Christ. An **antiques market** takes place in the cathedral's Piazza di San Martino on the third weekend of every month. Next to the cathedral is the state-of-the-art **Museo della Cattedrale** (*open 10–6 daily exc Mon; winter 10–1, 3–6, closed Mon*), holding some of its treasures, including the ornaments (the crown and garments) of the *Volto Santo*, tapestries and paintings from Lucca's ancient cathedral, San Giovanni, and della Quercia's St John the Evangelist.

Beyond the cathedral Piazza del Giglio leads to **Piazza Napoleone**, focus of the Lucchesi evening *passeggiata*. Via Vittorio Veneto leads from Piazza Napoleone into **Piazza San Michele**. San Michele itself was built about the same time as the cathedral, its full name, San Michele in Foro, coming from its location on what was Roman Lucca's forum. The ambitious façade rises high above the level of the roof, and every column in the Pisan arcading is different; some doubled, others twisted like corkscrews, inlaid with mosaic Cosmati work, or carved with monsters. The whole is crowned by a

san michele. lucca

giant statue of the Archangel. Inside, there's a glazed terracotta *Madonna and Child* attributed to Luca della Robbia, a striking 13th-century crucifixion over the high altar and a painting of plague saintsby Filippino Lippi. Giacomo Puccini began his musical career as a choirboy in San Michele (his father and grandfather had been organists in the cathedral)—he didn't have far to go, as he was born in Via di Poggio 30, just across the street. The house is now a little **Puccini Museum** (*entrance in Corte San Lorenzo 9, open summer 10–1, 3–6; winter 11–1, 3–5, closed Mon*), with memorabilia and the piano he used to compose *Turandot.*

East of San Michele, medieval **Via Fillungo** and its surrounding lanes make up the busy **shopping district**, a tidy nest of straight and narrow alleys. Along Via Fillungo you can trace the old *loggias* of the 14th-century palaces, now bricked in, and the ancient Torre delle Ore (tower of hours) which since 1471 has striven to keep the Lucchesi on time, and perhaps now suggests thst it's time for a coffee in the venerable Art Nouveau Caffè di Simo at No.58. At Via Fillungo's northern end stands the tall church and taller campanile of **San Frediano**, built in the early 1100s, and shimmering with the colours of the large mosaic on its upper façade. The 11th-century bronze Arabian falcon at the top is a copy—the original is so valuable that it is locked away in a safe. The palatial interior houses Tuscany's most remarkable baptismal font, the 12th-century *Fontana lustrale* carved with reliefs. The bedecked mummy is of St Zita, patroness of maids and ladies-in-waiting. Next to San Frediano, on Via Battisti, the **Palazzo Pfanner** (open *10–6 April–Oct; adm*) has a pretty 18th-century garden, a fine staircase, a collection of silks made in Lucca, and 17th–19th-century costumes. In the other direction, skirting Via Fillungo, narrow arches lead into something most visitors miss, the **Roman Amphitheatre**. Only outlines of its arches are still traceable in the outer walls, but Lucca is a city that changes so gradually and organically that the outline has been perfectly preserved. The foundations of the grandstands now support a perfect ellipse of medieval houses. Now, where gladiators once slugged it out, there is a wonderfully atmospheric piazza, where the boys play football and the less active sit musing in the sleepy cafés.

A Cure in Montecatini

Northwest of Florence, just west of Pistoia, lies the Valdinievole (literally 'cloudy valley'), a land obsessed with water, though mostly of the subterranean, curative variety. The Valdinievole's largest town, Montecatini Terme, is Italy's most glamorous thermal spa. Leonardo da Vinci's first drawing was of a view towards Montecatini from Lamporecchio, and he even designed a fountain for the baths of Montecatini in one of his notebooks, which after 380 years is currently being built of Carrara marble as his monument.

It is the despair of the Montecatini tourist board that Anglo-Saxons from both sides of the Atlantic refuse to believe that soaking in or drinking mere water can do anything as beneficial for them as imbibing a pitcher of Chianti. But it's important to remember that taking the waters, no matter how hot, radioactive or chock-full of minerals they may be, is only half the cure; the other is simply to relax, to stroll through gardens, listen to a little music, linger in a café, to indulge in a bit of the old *dolce far niente*. And in Montecatini (pop. 21,500) you can do just that without touching a blessed, unfermented drop. A leisurely lunch in a good old-fashioned restaurant like Enoteca Giovanni is the best way to begin a wallow in Belle Epoque nostalgia, strolling about and imagining the days when the spa seethed with dukes, politicians, literati and actresses; you may recognise it from Nikita Mikhalhov's film *Oci Ciornie*, starring Marcello Mastroianni.

getting there

Once in the town, follow signs for the railway station (there are two, you want the furthest west, near Piazza XX Settembre). There is a car park here. From the railway station, walk up Via Ricasoli, and take the second left, Via Garibaldi. Enoteca Giovanni is a narrow-fronted establishment on the first block.

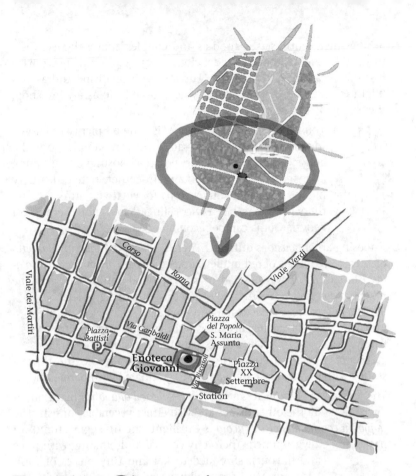

Enoteca Giovanni

Via Garibaldi 25, Montecatini Terme, © (0572) 71695. Closed Mon.
L75,000 excluding wine, all credit cards.

This is one of those Italian restaurants that you'd probably walk past if
you didn't know about it, dismissing it as prissily provincial after one
glimpse of its pastel flowery walls and pink and white napery.
Appearances, however, are deceiving, for Giovanni's is one of those
rare restaurants which manages to be relaxed and unpretentious
yet impeccably professional, attracting a busy lunchtime crowd of

businessmen, enthusiastic foodies and couples giving themselves a treat. What's more, the food is delicious, creative and intelligent, with just the occasional nod towards Tuscan traditionalism. And as you might expect from an operation which started life as a wine shop, there's a good choice of wine.

If you want help with the wine list, there's plenty of knowledgeable help on hand—and you can sample both the house Chiantis if you like, before choosing: one is young and springy, the other an altogether richer, leathery number. For both you pay only for what you drink. Among the whites, the tart Livio Felluga Sauvignon from Friuli Venezia Giulia can be recommended.

Choosing an *antipasto* is difficult. There's a *filetti di triglia in guazzetto* (gently stewed fillets of red mullet), *insalata tiepida di gamberetti e calamari* (a succulent warm salad of shrimps and squid), and *storione marinato con rucola* (marinated sturgeon with rocket). The *insalata di asparagi e tonno* (tuna and asparagus salad) we had was delicious, with generous slices of juicy tuna and young, barely cooked asparagus in a tangy balsamic dressing. The *fiori di zucca ripieni* (stuffed courgette flowers) are also good, the flowers stuffed with potato, basil and garlic and gratinated with parmesan.

The only pasta with meat is a *maccheroni al ragú di anatra* (macaroni in duck ragu)—all the other dishes are with either vegetables or fish. The *tagliolini con gamberetti e rucola* is excellent, the fine eggy strands of pasta tangled with prawns (perfectly cooked and bursting with juice and flavour), shredded rocket and tiny pieces of fresh tomato. Mushroom addicts will be kept happy with the *pennette con funghi porcini*, the slender pasta tubes glistening in a garlicky sauce of various ceps. Other choices include *tagliolini con polpa di granchio* (tagliolini with crab meat), *risotto con zucchine e zafferano* (courgette and saffron risotto) and *spaghetti alle vongole veraci* (spaghetti with clams).

Secondi are equally divided between meat and fish. The *carpaccio di manzo con rucola e parmigiano* (carpaccio with rocket and parmesan) is a good light choice, and the *rognone di vitello* (veal kidneys) wonderfully tender. If you want something richer, try the *piccione disossato*

(boned pigeon cooked with raisins and pine nuts) or the *petto di anatra ai grani di senape* (duck breast with mustard seed). If you prefer your meat grilled, there are grilled steaks and lamb cutlets.

As for fish, you could share a sea-bass (*branzino*) grilled, or, more unusually, *all'isolana*, baked with with potatoes, green olives, tomato and basil. Otherwise, there is *filetto di sanpietro con fiori di zucca* (John Dory with courgette flowers) or *filetto di sogliola alla vernaccia* (sole cooked in Vernaccia di San Gimignano).

Desserts are dangerously tempting, wheeled in on a trolley. If they have it, try *castagnaccio*, an unusual, almost savoury, grainy cake made of chestnut flour, pine nuts and rosemary, best eaten with a glass of *vin santo*.

Tagliolini con Gamberetti e Rucola

Serves 2

1 tablespoon extra virgin olive oil
1 clove garlic, crushed
100g/4oz fresh prawns, peeled and deveined
1 tablespoon dry white wine
200g/7oz fresh tagliolini
1 tablespoon parsley, finely chopped
1 bunch rocket, finely chopped
salt and pepper

Heat the oil in a pan, add the garlic and cook gently for a few minutes. Chop half the prawns and leave the rest whole. Add all the prawns to the pan with the wine and cook for about three minutes, until pink. Meanwhile, cook the tagiolini in a large pan of boiling salted water until al dente. Drain the pasta and stir into the prawns, then stir in the parsley and rocket. Season to taste and serve immediately.

touring around

A short stroll up from Enoteca Giovanni, past Montecatini's trendy boutiques, cafés, cinemas and some of its 200 hotels to Via Verdi, will take you into Montecatini's mineral water Elysium, the immaculately groomed **Parco delle Terme**, where the high temples of the cult dot the shaded lawn. The Lorraine grand dukes, spa-soaks like their Habsburg cousins, were behind the initial development of Montecatini's springs, and many of the baths, or *terme*, are neoclassical pavilions—monumental, classical and floral architecture that lent itself nicely to the later Liberty-style embellishments of the 1920s. Among these Art Nouveau fancies is Montecatini's **Municipio**, on Via Verdi opposite the park, or in the most sumptuous and ancient of its nine major bathing establishments, **Tettuccio**. In the 1370s a group of Florentines attempted to extract mineral salts from the spring and built a little roof (or *tettuccio*) over it; and although they failed it was soon discovered that the water had a good effect on rotten livers—one of the first to come here was Francesco Datini, the famous Merchant of Prato, in 1401. By the 18th century, Tettuccio was in a state of ruin, and Grand Duke Leopold I had it splendidly rebuilt. His façade remains, while the interior was redone by Montecatini's greatest architect, Ugo Giovanozzi, in the 1920s, embellished with paintings by Italy's Art Nouveau master, Galileo Chini, and ceramic pictures by Cascella in the drinking gallery; there's an elegant café, fountains, a reflecting pool and rotunda, writing hall, music rooms, a little city within a city—all adorned with scenes from an aquatic Golden Age of languid nymphs.

Other establishments, each with their special virtues, are nearby—the Palladian-style arcade of the Regina spring; the **Terme Leopoldine**, another grand ducal establishment, with mud baths housed in a temple-like building dedicated to Aesculapius, the god of health; the half-neo-Renaissance, half-modern **New Excelsior** baths; the pretty Tuscan rustic **Tamerici**, in its lush garden; the **Torretta**, with its phony medieval tower and afternoon concerts in the *loggia* (*baths open May–October, except for the Excelsior, which stays open all year*).

There is, however, more to Montecatini than water. There's the **Art Academy**, consisting solely of donations from Montecatini's

montecatini Terme

admirers—the piano Verdi used during his annual stays in the Locanda Maggiore, where he composed *Otello*, and art by Salvador Dali, Galileo Chini, Fattori and many others. There's another wooded park to explore, just behind the Parco delle Terme, called **Le Panteraie** (with a swimming-pool), where deer roam freely; you can sip an elegant coffee at the **Gran Caffè Gambrinus**, or perhaps play a round at the beautiful **Montecatini Golf Course**, set among olive groves and cypresses, © 62 218, or a game of tennis at the courts in Via dei Bari, © 767 587/5; or try to win back your hotel bill at the trotting races at the **Ippodromo**. The **Circolo dei Forestieri** (foreigners' club) and the **Kursaal** (with cinema, night-club, games) are popular meeting places. One of the prettiest excursions is to take the funicular up to **Montecatini Alto**, the original old hill town, with breathtaking views over the Valley of Mists and a charming little piazza with a charming little theatre; nearby you can visit the stalactites in the **Grotta Maona** (*open April–Oct*).

On the other hand, lovely narrow lanes crisscross the Valdiniecole landscape, offering tempting excursions further afield. Five km east of Montecatini is its sister spa, **Monsummano Terme**, offering vapour baths in natural grottoes. The first of these strange caves was discovered by accident in 1849, when the Giusti family moved a boulder and found the entrance to a stalactite cave, the **Grotta Giusti** (*open April–Nov*), 100m deep, with three small lakes fed by hot springs; a second steamy cave, the **Grotta Parlanti** (*open May–Oct; information ℗ (0572) 51029*), is used for serious treatments. Monsummano, however, hasn't rested on its vapours, but has transformed itself into one of Italy's biggest shoemaking towns; like Montecatini it has an old antecedent atop a hill, Monsummano Alto, all but abandoned these days, but with a pretty Romanesque church, a romantically ruined castle and splendid views. Another panoramic view may be had from **Montevettolini**, 4km from Monsummano, site of a villa built by Ferdinando I in 1597.

If you prefer your castles more intact, continue east to the old fortress at **Serravalle Pistoiese**, which, as its name translates, 'locks the valley' between the Apennines and Monte Albano. Its old Lombard tower and 14th-century additions saw considerable action in Tuscany's days of inter-urban hooliganism.

To the west of Montecatini, there's another attractive old hilltown, **Buggiano Castello**, and for those who imagine that fresco went out of fashion years ago, there's San Michele in nearby **Ponte Buggianese**, freshly frescoed in stark colours by Pietro Annigoni. The colours are even more dazzling in **Pescia** (pop. 20,000), Italy's capital of flowers, a title this little city with a green thumb has snatched from San Remo on the Riviera. Some three million cut flowers are sent off every day in the summer from Pescia's giant market; besides carnations, lilies and gladioli, it is celebrated by gourmets for its tender asparagus and its *fagioli* (white beans).

Pescia has a number of interesting monuments, beginning with a 14th-century church of **San Francesco**, containing a portrait of St Francis with scenes from his life, painted in 1235 by Bonaventura Berlinghieri and considered to be one of the most authentic likenesses of the saint; also be sure to take a look at the Crucifixion by Puccio Capanna in the sacristy. The **Duomo** was rebuilt in the 1600s, but has a fine Romanesque campanile wearing its little cupola like a beanie, and a late terracotta triptych by Luca della Robbia. On the long, narrow Piazza Mazzini stands the imposing **Palazzo del Vicario**, with the usual mishmash of stone escutcheons; in nearby **Sant'Antonio**, built in the 1360s, look up the 'Ugly Saints', a 13th-century wood *Deposition from the Cross*.

More than a Leaning Tower

Pisa is at once the best-known and the most mysterious of Tuscan cities. Its most celebrated attraction, the Leaning Tower, has become, along with the Colosseum, gondolas and spaghetti, a symbol for the entire Italian republic.

Tour of buses disgorge thousands daily into the Field of Miracles before moving on to Florence, Elba or Rome; at night even the Pisani make a mass exodus into the suburbs. Yet go back to about 1100 and precious Pisa was, according to the chronicles, 'the city of marvels', the 'city of 10,000 towers', with a population of 300,000. Pisan merchants made themselves at home all over the Mediterranean, bringing back new ideas and new styles in art in addition to their profit. Pisan Romanesque, with its stripes and blind arcades, was inspired by the great Moorish architecture of Andalucía, and Nicola Pisano, first of a long line of great sculptors, is as important to the Renaissance of sculpture as Giotto is to painting.

Kiss of Judas. detail from Cathedral doors

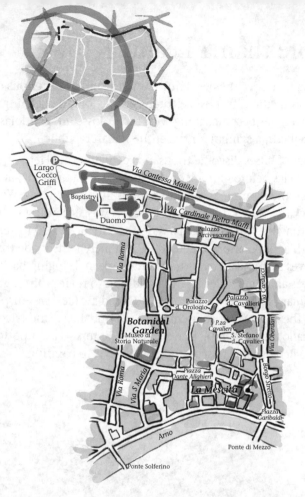

Like a Middle Eastern city, Pisa has put all its efforts into one fabulous spiritual monument, while the rest of the city wears a decidedly undemonstrative, almost anonymous face, a little run-down. The most charismatic part of town is undoubtedly the bustling morning product market directly outside La Mescita, so to make the most of Pisa, see the Field of Miracles, wander around the market before lunch, then walk off lunch along the Arno.

Park on Largo Cocco Griffi, behind the Baptistry, and wander through the Campo dei Miracoli to Via Cardinale Pietro Maffi. Then turn right down the bustling main street, Via Carducci, which shortly changes its name to Via Oberdan, and then Borgo Stretto. Take the second alleyway on the right, and you'll come to the produce market which centres on arcaded Piazza Vettovaglie. La Mescita is just off the square on Via Cavalca, half hidden behind a vegetable stall.

La Mescita

Via Cavalca 2, Pisa, © (050) 544294. Closed Saturday lunch and Sun, 2 weeks August. L30,000, L35,000, all credit cards.

Marketplace *trattorias* are a long-established Italian tradition, most of them rough-and-ready places, where stallholders and workers congregate at long wooden tables to knock back jugs of local plonk and devour mountains of pasta. La Mescita is quite different. Once you have negotiated the cabbage leaves, squashed peaches and cartons of borlotti beans outside, the bawdy bustle of the market is forgotten. Instead, you find yourself in a serene vaulted room, where you are greeted by a campish waiter in jeans and a shirt, and led to a table laid with aqua brocade and strange tropical flowers.

Perhaps the secret of La Mescita is that it is owned by its chef, Marco Griffo, whose flair, intelligence and attention to detail suffuses every aspect of the place. As soon as you are settled with menu and wine list, a basket of breads is brought: cubes of *focaccia* and slices of coarse wholewheat country bread from the bakery across the street. The wine list is huge, wide-ranging and well-informed, with an emphasis on new-wave Italian wines. Unless you know your stuff, it's as well to let the waiter help you choose something to go with your food. The Terre di Tufi, a perfumed Vernaccia di San Gimignano, recommended to go with the light summery dishes we ordered, was just right.

The food is wonderful. Not only is everything seasonal and absolutely fresh, but Marco is one of those rare cooks with a genuine sensitivity to his ingredients. If they're on the menu, try the *fiori di zucca*, courgette flowers stuffed with tepid herb-scented ricotta and served with diced tomatoes and fine strips of basil: for once you actually have the sensation of eating a flower, not an unidentifiable deepfried shrivel.

You could follow this with one of the *tagliolini* dishes—a huge plate of delicate puckering pasta ribbons served with *gamberetti, piselli e* *asparagi* (prawns, peas and asparagus), *vongole veraci* (clams), *carciofi* (artichokes), *bottarga* (sturgeons' eggs) or even *cima di rapa* (turnip tops) and goat's cheese.

Most interesting of the secondi are the delicous *insalata calda di baccalà con pomodoro, patate e ceci* (a warm salad of salt cod with potato, tomato and chickpeas) and the *faraona dissossata al carciofo* (boned guinea fowl with artichokes), but there are also more simple dishes like grilled fish and steak. If your appetite is flagging you could always nip back to the *antipasti*, for a plate of smoked fish or a *sformato di porri con salsa di fagioli* (a delicate mousse of leeks with a white bean sauce). There are also huge salads (including Greek). Desserts range from a healthy Greek yogurt with honey and pine nuts to a more indulgent *panna cotta al cioccolato.*

As well as being able to pick and choose *à la carte*, there are three excellent-value set menus, one vegetarian (L30,000), one meat-based (L30,000) and one fish (L35,000), all of them including a dessert.

Tagliolini con Gamberetti, Piselli e Asparagi

Serves 2

1 tablespoon extra virgin olive oil
1 clove garlic, crushed
100g/4oz fresh prawns, peeled and deveined
1 tablespoon dry white wine
100g/4oz fresh peas, lightly cooked
6 asparagus spears, lightly cooked and chopped
200g/7oz fresh tagliolini
1 tablespoon chopped parsley
salt and pepper

Heat the oil in a pan, add the garlic and cook gently for a few minutes. Chop half the prawns and leave the rest whole. Add all the prawns to the pan with the wine and cook for about three minutes, until pink. Stir in the peas and asparagus and heat through gently. Meanwhile, cook the tagiolini in a large pan of boiling salted water until al dente. Drain the pasta and stir into the sauce, then add the parsley. Season to taste and serve immediately.

touring around

Almost from the time of its conception, medieval Italy's most ambitious building programme was given the nickname of the '**Field of Miracles**'. Of all the unique things about this complex, the location strikes one first. Whether their reasons had to do with aesthetics or land values—probably a little of both—the Pisans built their cathedral on a broad expanse of green lawn at the northern edge of town, just inside the walls. The cathedral was begun in 1063, the famous Leaning Tower and the baptistry in the middle 1100s, at the height of Pisa's fortunes, and the Campo Santo in 1278. (*For the museums and monuments on the* campo, *you can save by getting the joint ticket, for L15,000*).

The **Baptistry** (*open 9am–sunset*) is the biggest of its kind in Italy; those of many other cities would fit neatly inside. The original architect, with the felicitous name of Master Diotisalvi ('God save you'), saw the lower half of the building done in the typical stripes-and-arcades Pisan style. A second colonnade was intended to go over the first, but as the Genoese gradually muscled Pisa out of trade routes, funds ran short. In the 1260s, Nicola and Giovanni Pisano redesigned and completed the upper half in a harmonious Gothic crown of gables and pinnacles. The Pisanos also added the dome over Diotisalvi's original prismatic dome, still visible from the inside.

Inside, the austerity of the simple, striped walls and heavy columns of grey Elban granite is broken by the great 13th-century baptismal font, the work of Guido Bigarelli, who made the crazy pulpit in Barga. There is little figurative sculpture on it, but the sixteen exquisite marble panels are finely carved in floral and geometrical patterns of inlaid stones. The baptistry is famous for its uncanny acoustics; if you have the place to yourself, try singing a few notes from as near to centre as they will allow you. If there's a crowd the guards will be just waiting for someone to bribe them to do it.

One of the first and finest works of the Pisan Romanesque, the façade of the **cathedral** (*open 7.45–1 and 3–sunset, closed to tourists for church services; adm*), with four levels of colonnades, turned out to be a little more ornate than Buscheto, the architect, had planned back in 1063. These columns, with similar colonnades around the apse and the Gothic frills later added around the unique elliptical dome, are the only showy features on the calm, restrained exterior. On the south transept, the late 12th-century Porte San Ranieri has a fine pair of bronze doors by Bonanno, one of the architects of the Leaning Tower. The Biblical scenes are enacted among real palms and acacia trees; naturally, the well-travelled Pisans would have known what such things looked like.

On the inside, little of the original art survived a fire in 1595, but some fine work survives. The great mosaic of *Christ Pantocrator* in the apse is by Cimabue, and there are portraits of the saints by Andrea del Sarto in the choir and his *Madonna della Grazia* on the right nave. The pulpit (*c.* 1300), by Giovanni Pisano, is the acknowledged masterpiece of the family. The men of 1595 used the fire as an opportunity to get rid of this nasty old medieval relic, and the greatest achievement of Pisan sculpture sat disassembled in crates, quite forgotten until this century. Pisano's pulpit is startling, mixing classical and Christian elements with a fluency never seen before his time. St Michael, as a telamon, shares the honour of supporting the pulpit with Hercules and the Fates, while prophets, saints and sibyls look on from their appointed places. The relief panels, jammed with expressive faces, diffuse an electric immediacy equal to the best work of the Renaissance. Notice particularly the *Nativity*, the *Massacre of the Innocents*, the *Flight into Egypt*, and the *Last Judgement*.

Behind the cathedral is the familiar silhouette of the **Leaning Tower**. The stories claiming the tilt was accidental were most likely pure fabrications to account for what, before mass tourism, must have seemed a great civic embarrassment. The argument isn't very convincing. It seems hard to believe that the tower would start to lean when only 10m tall; half the weight would still be in the foundations. The argument then insists that the Pisans doggedly kept building it after the lean commenced. The architects who measured the stones in the last century to get to the bottom of the mystery concluded that the tower's odd state was absolutely intentional from the day it was begun in 1173. Mention this to a Pisan, and he will be as offended as if you had suggested lunacy is a problem in his family.

In recent years the tilt began to increase to around 1mm per year, and in 1993 work began on securing the tower. the first stage involved ballasting the base of the tilting side with lead. Now, the lead is being replaced by underground steel cables. The weights alone have succeeded in reversing the tilt by 1.5mm per year.

If one more marvel in the Campo dei Miracoli is not excessive, there is this remarkable cloister of the **Campo Santo**, as unique in its way as the Leaning Tower (*open 9–5 Oct–Mar; 8–8 April–Sept; adm*). Basically, the cemetery is a rectangle of gleaming white marble, unadorned save for the blind arcading around the façade and the beautiful Gothic tabernacle of the enthroned Virgin Mary over the entrance. With its uncluttered, simple lines, the Campo Santo seems more like a work of our own century than the 1300s.

The cemetery began, according to legend, when Archbishop Lanfranchi, who led the Pisan fleet into the Crusades, came back with boatloads of soil from the Holy Land for extra-blessed burials. Over the centuries an exceptional hoard of frescoes and sculpture accumulated here. Much of it went up in flames in July 1944, when an Allied incendiary bomb hit the roof and set it on fire. Many priceless works of art were destroyed and others, including most of the frescoes, damaged beyond hope of ever being perfectly restored. The biggest loss, perhaps, was the set of frescoes by Benozzo Gozzoli—the *Tower of Babylon*, *Solomon and Sheba*, *Life of Moses* and the *Grape Harvest* and others; in their original state they must have been as fresh and colourful as his famous frescoes in Florence's Medici Palace. Even better known, and better preserved, are two 14th-century frescoes of the *Triumph of Death* and the *Last Judgement* by an unknown artist (perhaps Andrea Orcagna of Florence).

After the Campo dei Miracoli, the thing that has most impressed Pisa's visitors is its languidly curving stretch of the Arno, an exercise in

Tuscan gravity, the river lined with two mirror-image lines of blank-faced yellow and tan buildings, all the same height, with no remarkable bridges or any of the picturesque quality of Florence. Its uncanny monotony is broken by only one landmark, but it is something special. Near the Solferino Bridge, **Santa Maria della Spina** sits on the bank like a precious Gothic jewel-box. Though one of the few outstanding achievements of Italian Gothic, originally it wasn't Gothic at all. Partially rebuilt in 1323, its new architect—perhaps one of the Pisanos—turned it into an extravaganza of pointed gables and blooming pinnacles. All of the sculptural work is first class, especially the figures of Christ and the Apostles in the thirteen niches facing the streets. The chapel takes its name from a thorn of Christ's crown of thorns, a relic brought back from the Crusades.

Only a few blocks west, near the walls where the famous 'Golden Gate'—medieval Pisa's door to the sea—once stood, remains of the old Citadel and Arsenal are still visible across the river. On the southern side, **San Paolo a Ripa del Arno** has an interesting 12th-century façade similar to that of the cathedral. San Paolo stands in a small park, and interestingly it is believed to have been built over the site of Pisa's original cathedral; perhaps building cathedrals in open fields was an old custom. Behind it the unusual and very small 12th-century chapel of **Sant'Agata** has eight sides and an eight-sided prismatic roof like an Ottoman tomb. Just across Ponte Solferino, behind the Palazzo Reale, is the large church of **San Nicola**, with a fine painting of the *Madonna* by Traini, a sculpture of the same by Nino Pisano, and a painting of St Nicholas of Toletino shielding Pisa from the plague. Ask the sacristan to show you the famous spiral stair in the 13th-century campanile.

Down the Arno, the monotony is briefly broken again by the arches of the 17th-century **Logge di Banchi**, the old silk and wool market, at the Ponte di Mezzo and at the head of Pisa's main shopping street, Corso Italia. A bit further down is another octagonal church, **San Sepolcro**, built originally for the Knights Templar by Diotisalvi. **Palazzo Lanfranchi** further down is used for exhibitions. There's a small but shady park in the former Bastion Sangallo.

Munching with the Medici

The Medici of the Renaissance were formidable gastronomes, and the batallions of cooks they employed did much to refine and develop the cuisine of Florence and its environs. For a start, the Medici men married women from all over Europe: thus Spanish influences were introduced by Eleonora of Toledo, wife of Cosimo I, Roman by Clarice Orsini, wife of Lorenzo il Magnifico, and Austrian by Giovanna of Austria, first wife of Francesco I. The marriage of Lorenzo and Clarice in 1469 was celebrated by no less than five banquets, and for weeks beforehand gifts of game, poultry, wine, cakes, jellies, sweetmeats, marzipan and sugared almonds flooded in from all over Tuscany. And when Giovanni de' Medici became Pope Leo X in 1513, he took his taste for lavish banqueting with him, and soon became famed not only for serving such delicacies as peacocks' tongues, but for extravagant surprises, such as nightingales flying out of pies, and naked children leaping out of huge puddings. Catherine de' Medici almost died from eating too much *cibrèo*, a kind of pâté, but was also responsible for introducing artichokes and béchamel sauce to Paris when

Da Delfina

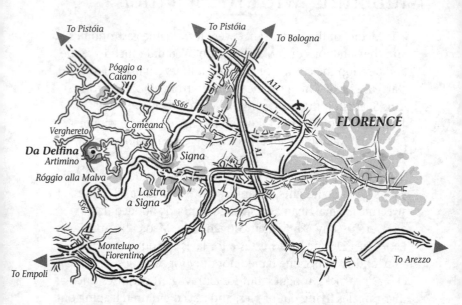

she became wife to Henri II of France at the age of 14. In Tuscany the sauce was known unappealingly as *colla*, glue; in France it was renamed after a courtier, Louis de Béchameil).

The countryside outside Florence is littered with Medici villas. Like their Bourbon cousins in France, the Medici dukes liked to pass the time acquiring new palaces for themselves. In their case, however, the reason was less self-exaltation than simple property speculation; the Medici always thought several generations ahead. Although most of the villas are now privately owned, some are at least partly open to the public. Two of the most interesting, Poggio a Caiano and Villa Artimino, lie to the west of Florence. This is a chance for a lazy day out in the company of the Medici, with lunch in an appropriately refined restaurant where you can eat on a terrace overlooking the extraordinary Renaissance Villa Artimino.

Approaching Artimino from the south, drive straight through the village. The restaurant is just beyond the village walls, on a ridge overlooking the villa of Artimino.

Da Delfina

*Via della Chiesa 1, Località Artimino, nr Carmignano, ℗ (0558) 718074.
Closed Mon eve and Tues, hols August. L55,000, no credit cards.*

Da Delfina is a refined, serene and romantic restaurant in a pretty *casa colonica* perched on the lip of a hill. It is at its best in spring or summer, when you can sit on the terrace outside and look across the vine-ridged hills to the Villa of Artimino. Though it is not particularly expensive, such care is taken with the food, service and atmosphere that you feel it must be—it is certainly somewhere to bear in mind for a special occasion. The food is excellent, the result of a fertile relationship between traditional Tuscan fare and the imagination of the chef, with the emphasis on top-quality ingredients (hand-made pasta, local traditionally raised meat, seasonal vegetables and fruit). What's more, for once in an upscale restaurant, the service—by locals—seems designed to put you at your ease rather than intimidate.

The wines come from all over Italy, so there are some of the delicious northern whites (lots from the excellent Jermann vineyards in Friuli) and Piedmontese as well as Tuscan reds. The menu changes according to season, but is always full of temptations. You might find a salad of white beans and pine nuts, a chicken liver mousse, or simply a selection of *prosciutto* and *finocchiona*. Even the *crostini* are interesting, with deftly seasoned chicken liver pâté spread on a thin slice of *polenta*, or an artichoke heart stuffed with buffalo *mozzarella*. Another winner is the *sformato di ortiche*, a delicate, creamy and nicely textured nettle mould, surrounded by a subtle puree of pumpkin.

For a *primo* there might be a tasty *ribollita* so thick you can stand your spoon upright in it, hand-made *ravioli* in a sauce of creamed aubergines, or a delicous *farfalle* with peppers. But the truly unmissable dish is *gnocchi alla parietaria*, perfect melt-in-the-mouth gnocchi dressed with melted butter and a local herb known as *parietaria* because it grows on walls (*parete*).

Secondi are no disappointment, with the excellence of the meat—elderly Tuscans insists it tastes the way it used to when they were young—matching the skills of the chef (who knows when and when not to intervene). *Scottadito* are young juicy, grilled lamb chops and *capretto*, extremely young kid, is delicate, unbelievably tender and scented with wood from the oven in which it was roasted. Lighter

dishes include a fantastic *fritto di formaggio e verdure*, feather-light bubbles of battered cheese and vegetables, and *melanzane ai funghi*, velvety aubergine stuffed with mushrooms. Do have a salad to accompany your *secondi*: even the green salad has inspired additions like mint, perfect, of course, if you're having lamb.

Desserts change from day to day. One utterly brilliant creation is a recipe to remember: a crunchy, creamy dollop of yogurt mixed with cooked cream, crushed *amaretti* biscuits, honey and liqueur and topped with cherries, raspberries and miniature wild strawberries. If you've still room, nibble a selection of unusually pliant *cantucci*, airy *berlingozza* and knobbly almondy *brutti e buoni*, dipped in a glass (or two) of one of Da Delfina's many dessert wines.

Melanzane ai Funghi

Serves 4

4 medium aubergines
2 tablespoons extra virgin olive oil
3 cloves garlic, crushed
1 bunch basil, chopped
400g/14oz mixed wild mushrooms (preferably including porcini, chopped)
200g/7oz tomatoes, skinned and chopped
25g/1oz Parmesan cheese, freshly grated
salt and pepper

Cut the aubergines in half lengthways and scoop out the insides. Chop the flesh. Sprinkle the aubergine shells with salt and turn upside down to drain. Set aside while you make the filling.

Heat the olive oil in a frying pan, add the garlic and basil and cook gently for a minute. Add the mushrooms, aubergine flesh and tomatoes and simmer for about 5 minutes, until thick. Season to taste.

Rinse and dry the aubergine shells and fill with the mushroom mixture. Sprinkle with the Parmesan and bake in an oven preheated to 200°C/400°F (gas mark 6) for about 30 minutes until brown on top.

---

touring around

The Etruscan city of **Artimino** was destroyed by the Romans and is now occupied by a small town and another Medici property, the **Villa Artimino** ('La Ferdinanda'), built as hunting lodge for Ferdinando I by Buontalenti. Buontalenti gave it a semi-fortified air with buttresses to fit its sporting purpose, but the total effect is simple and charming, the long roofline punctuated by innumerable chimneys; the graceful stair was added in the last century from a drawing by the architect in the Uffizi. An **Etruscan Archaeological Museum** has been installed in the basement, containing items found in the tombs; among them a unique censer with two basins and a boat, bronze vases, and a red fig-ured krater painted with initiation scenes, found in a 3rd-century tomb (*villa open only by appointment, © 879 2030; museum open 9–12.30 Mon–Sun closed Wed; adm*). Also in Artimino is an attractive Romanesque church, **San Leonardo**, built of stones salvaged from earlier buildings.

Four km east, at **Comeana** is the well-preserved Etruscan **Tomba di Montefortini** (*open 9–12, closed Wed*), a 7th-century BC burial mound, 11m high and 80m in diameter, covering two burial chambers. A long hall leads down to the vestibule and rectangular tomb chamber, both carefully covered with false vaulting, the latter preserving a wide shelf, believed to have been used for gifts for the afterlife. An equally impressive tomb nearby, the **Tomba dei Boschetti** (*open 9–12, closed Wed*), was seriously damaged over the centuries by local farmers.

Of all the Medici villas, **Poggio a Caiano** (*open 9–12.30, 3–4.30, Sun 9–2.30, closed Mon; adm*) is the most evocative of the country idylls so delightfully described in the verses of Lorenzo il Magnifico; this was his favourite retreat (*℗ 877 012, COPIT buses go past every half-hour, departing from the loggia in Florence's Piazza Santa Maria Novella*). Originally a farmhouse purchased by Lorenzo in 1480, it was rebuilt by Giuliano da Sangallo in a classical style that presages Palladio. It was Lorenzo's sole architectural commission, and its classicism matched the mythological nature poems he composed here, most famously L'Ambra, inspired by the nearby stream Ombrone.

Sangallo designed the villa according to Alberti's description of the perfect country house, and added a classical frieze on the façade, sculpted with the assistance of Andrea Sansovino (now replaced with a copy). Some of the other features—the clock, the curved stair and central *loggia*—were later additions. In the **interior** Sangallo designed an airy, two-storey *salone*, which the two Medici popes had frescoed by 16th-century masters Pontormo, Andrea del Sarto, Franciabigio and Allori. The subject, as usual, is Medici self-glorification, and depicts family members dressed as Romans in historical scenes that parallel events in their lives. In the right lunette, around a large circular window, Pontormo painted the lovely Vertumnus and Pomona (1521), a languid summer scene under a willow tree, beautifully coloured. The pleasant grounds contain many fine old trees and a 19th-century statue celebrating Lorenzo's L'Ambra.

A local bus continues 5km southwest of Poggia a Caiano to the village of **Carmignano**, which possesses in its church of San Michele Pontormo's uncanny painting of *The Visitation* (1530s), one of the masterpieces of Florentine Mannerism. There are no concessions to naturalism here—the four soulful, ethereal women, draped in Pontormo's accustomed startling colours, barely touch the ground, standing before a scene as substantial as a stage backdrop. The result is one of the most unforgettable images produced in the 16th century.

A Gastrodome at the Market

cibrio caffe

According to the tourist office, in 1993 a grand tour of 2,300,000 Americans, Germans, French, Britons and other foreigners as well as some 800,000 Italians spent at least one night in a Florentine hotel. Some, perhaps, came for orthodontist appointments; a large percentage of the others came to inhale the rarefied air of the cradle of Western civilization, to gaze at some of the loveliest things made by mortal hands and minds, to walk the streets of the new Athens, the great humanist 'city built to the measure of man'. Florence's museums, palaces and churches contain more good art than perhaps any city in Europe, and to see it all would take at least three weeks. If you have only a couple of days, you will probably want to focus on the highlights such as the cathedral, Uffizi, Accademia and so on; but if this is not your first visit and you're looking for something less hard on the eyes, feet and sensibilities, this day out is just a little different.

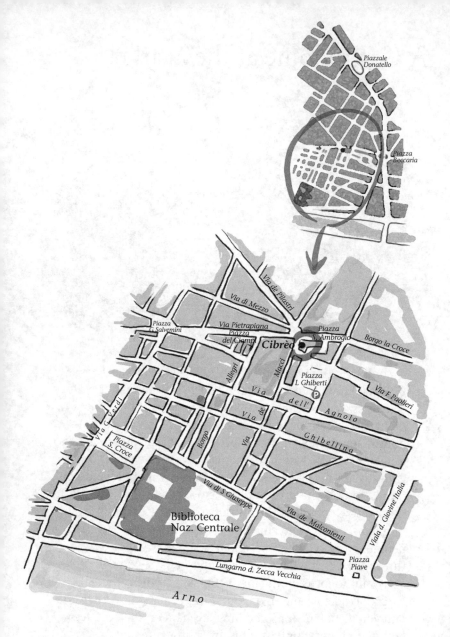

In an area of the city off the beaten tourist track, close to the fabulous Sant'Ambrogio produce market and the antiques and bric-a-brac shops on and around Piazza dei Ciompi, is Cibrèo, one of the most creative yet traditional restaurants in Tuscany, which has influenced chefs from Valentina Harris to Rose Grey and Ruth Rogers of London's River Café. The day is based around a lazy morning browsing in the antiques shops and market, with a good long walk to Santissima Annunziata after lunch, so you can work up an appetite for dinner.

getting there

Florence's one-way system makes getting to Cibrèo quite tricky. If you're on foot, however, it's a pleasant ten-minute walk from Piazza Santa Croce, heading up Borgo Allegri, then right along Via Pietrapiana. If you're driving in from outside Florence, head clockwisse around the ring road, passing the Fortezza da Basso (there are often signs for exhibitions held here, if you get confused), and through the large Piazza della Libertà to Viale Matteotti. Continue past the oval loop, Piazzale Donatello, and head down to Piazza Beccaria, taking any turn you are permitted to take to the right. Keep a sharp eye out for parking signs: the most convenient for the restaurant is on Piazza Ghiberti.

Cibrèo

Via dei Macci 118r, Florence, © (055) 234 1100. Closed Sun and Mon.
L65,000 excluding wine (restaurant), L40,000 excluding wine (trattoria),
all credit cards.

For anyone remotely interested in Tuscan food, lunch (and dinner, and lunch again) in Cibrèo is a must. There are two dining rooms: a simple tiled *trattoria* with four large marble-topped tables, where you cannot book and will probably have to share a table (with anyone from a lawyer or banker to stallholders from the market outside); and a serene wood-panelled room with an arcane selection of paintings, wood-cuts and posters on the wall. Here the service is superb—informed, responsive and intelligent—and prices are double. The food in both rooms is cooked in the small kitchen that lies between them, and there are many dishes in common, though the menu in the *trattoria* has a more limited selection of *secondi*, and a shorter wine list.

Arrive in the restaurant exhausted after a flight and flustered from negotiating Florence's traffic, and you are immediately soothed. Before you know it, there are glasses of white wine on the table, followed, an instant later, by a tantalising and generous assembly of *amuse-gueules* (there are no *antipasti*). The undisputed star is a soft tomato jelly—perfect melt-in-the-mouth texture, and deliciously spiced with basil and pepper. Also good is a ricotta and parmesan soufflé. There is also a tripe salad, thin strips of gelatinous tripe in a spicy dressing.

The most unusual (in Italy possibly unique) feature of Cibrèo is that there is no pasta on the menu. Even pasta addicts, however, will be swiftly cured by the fabulous soups, soufflés and polenta dishes on offer. They also use more chilli (*peperoncino*) than is common in most Tuscan restaurants, which is grown by chef Fabio Picchi's father, in his Florence garden. There is no written menu, so while you're nibbling your *amuse-gueules*, a waiter will come and tell you what there is. He or she will also guide you through the wine list if you need it: there are Tuscan reds and Chiantis aplenty, but, thankfully a refreshing selection of northern whites—the Friuli Celso del Ronco Sauvignon is a good lively, zingy lunchtime choice.

The yellow pepper soup (*passato di peperoni gialli*) is a masterpiece, mild, creamy and bursting with the flavour of fresh, sweet juicy peppers. It comes served with a hieroglyph of scrumptious olive oil and a miniature cascade of grated parmesan. Another winner is the potato and ricotta soufflé, light, delicate and gently spiced. There is also a great thick, flavoursome spicy fish soup, a great *pappa al pomodoro* (an aptly pappy bread and tomato soup), and on cold days, *ribollita*, with on warmer days a lighter version, *minestra di pane*, made with bread, tomato, white beans and white cabbage. If you like polenta, try the *polenta all'erbe*, cooked with dried herbs, and served with butter and parmesan.

To follow there might be fish simply cooked *al car-toccio* (in foil), pot-roast veal, stuffed duck breast or rabbit, spicy sausages served with cannellini beans and cabbage, shelled mussels cooked in butter, lambs brains, and *inzimino*, a gutsy Tuscan speciality. The *inzimino* is splendid, a pungent, spicy, juicy squid, spinach and chard stew served in a miniature metal pan with triangles of toast. The duck stuffed with

pine-nuts and raisins may be rather old-fashioned for some tastes—try the sausages, or the baked fish instead. Accompanying are unusual vegetables—*cavolfiori con salsicce*, a tasty fennel-seed-spiked mush of cauliflower and sausage, and *patate in umido*, steamed, mildly spicy potatoes.

For dessert there is usually a selection of *bavarese* (bavarois), various *torte* (try the bitter chocolate, *cioccolato amaro*) and a scrumptious *torta di pere*, a buttery concoction of pear, sultanas and pine-nuts in thin, sugar-crusted buttery pastry.

Passata di Peperoni Gialli

Serves 4–6

2 tablespoons extra virgin olive oil, plus extra to serve
1 red onion, finely chopped
1 carrot, finely chopped
1 stick celery, finely chopped
4 yellow peppers, coarsely chopped
4 medium potatoes, coarsely chopped
light meat stock or water
1 small glass full-fat milk
2 bay leaves
freshly grated Parmesan cheese
salt

Heat the oil in a pan, add the onion, carrot and celery and cook gently, stirring constantly. When the vegetables are soft and golden, add the peppers and potatoes, then pour in enough stock or water to cover generously. Salt sparingly and simmer for 25 minutes or until the potatoes are soft.

Purée the soup, then return to the pan, and add the milk and bay leaves and heat gently. The soup should not boil again or it will lose its colour. Taste for salt, then remove from the heat. Serve with a drizzle of good extra virgin olive oil and a sprinkling of parmesan cheese.

touring around

Sant'Ambrogio and the Flea Market

This is a forage into a little-known area of Florence, offering some respite from a cultural overload. To get the most out of it, start in the morning, so you can poke around in the flea market on Piazza dei Ciompi and the brilliant **produce market** on **Piazza di Sant' Ambrogio**. The streets in this quarter of the city are among the most dusty and piquant in the central Florence. Life revolves around the church of Sant'Ambrogio and its neighbouring food market made of cast iron in 1873; the **church** (rebuilt in the 13th century, 19th-century façade) is of interest for its fine works of art: the second chapel on the right has a lovely fresco of the *Madonna Enthroned with Saints* by Orcagna (or his school) and the Cappella del Miracolo, just left of the high altar, contains Mino da Fiesole's celebrated marble *Tabernacle* (1481) and his own tomb. The chapel has a fresco of a procession by Cosimo Rosselli, especially interesting for its depiction of 15th-century costume and its contemporary portraits. Andrea Verrocchio is

mercato centrale

buried in the fourth chapel on the left; on the wall by the second altar, there's a *Nativity* by Baldovinetti. The fresco of an atypical St Sebastian in the first chapel of the left is by Agnolo Gaddi.

From Sant'Ambrogio take Via Pietrapiana to the bustling **Piazza dei Ciompi**, named after the wool-workers' revolt of 1378. In the morning, Florence's **flea market** or **Mercatino** takes place here, the best place in town to buy that 1940s radio or outdated ballgown you've always wanted. One side of the square is graced with the **Loggia del Pesce**, built by Vasari in 1568 for the fishmongers of the Mercato Vecchio; when that was demolished the *loggia* was salvaged and re-erected here.

After lunch at Cibrèo, head into the heart of Jewish Florence. Florence's Jewish community, although today only 1200 strong, has long been one of the most important in Italy, invited to Florence by the Republic in 1430, but repeatedly exiled and readmitted until Cosimo I founded Florence's ghetto in 1551. When the ghetto was opened up in 1848 and demolished soon after, a new **synagogue** (1874–82) was built in Via L.C. Farini: a tall, charming Mozarabic Pre-Raphaelite hybrid inspired by the Hagia Sophia and the Transito Synagogue of Toledo (*security is tight, but the synagogue may be toured April–Sept, Sun–Thurs, 10–1 and 2–5; men must cover their heads*). Although seriously damaged by the Nazis in August 1944—and later by the Arno in 1966—it has been lovingly restored. There's a small **Jewish Museum** upstairs (*open same hours as synagogue, call © 245 252/3 for information*), with a documentary history of Florentine Jews as well as ritual and ceremonial items from the synagogue's treasure.

From here you could take look at one of the city's least known but most intriguing churches, **Santa Maria Maddalena dei Pazzi** (*open 9–12 and 5–7*), a fine example of architectural syncretism. The church itself was founded in the 13th century, rebuilt in classically Renaissance style by Giuliano da Sangallo, then given a full dose of Baroque when the church was rededicated to the Counter-Reformation saint of the Pazzi family. Inside it's all high theatre, with a gaudy **trompe-l'œil** ceiling, paintings by Luca Giordano, florid chapels, and a wild marble chancel. From the Sacristy a door leads down into a crypt full of mouldering ecclesiastics to the Chapter

House, which contains a fresco of the *Crucifixion* (1496), one of Perugino's masterpieces. Despite the symmetry and quiet, contemplative grief of the five figures at the foot of the Cross and the magic stillness of the luminous Tuscan-Umbrian landscape, the fresco has a powerful impact, giving the viewer the uncanny sensation of being able to walk right into the scene.

Santissima Annunziata

If you still need to walk off lunch,take the longish but worthwhile trek along dull Renaissance Via della Colonna, to end your walk in **Piazza Santissima Annunziata**. This lovely square, really the only Renaissance attempt at a unified ensemble in Florence, is surrounded on three sides by arcades. In its centre, gazing down the splendid vista of Via dei Servi towards the Duomo, stands the equestrian statue of Ferdinand I (1607) by Giambologna and his pupil Pietro Tacca, made of bronze from Turkish cannons captured during the Battle of Lepanto. More fascinating than Ferdinand are the pair of bizarre Baroque fountains, also by Tacca, that share the square. Though possessed of a marine theme, they resemble tureens of bouillabaisse.

In the 1420s Filippo Brunelleschi struck the first blow for classical calm in this piazza when he built the celebrated **Spedale degli Innocenti** and its famous portico—an architectural landmark, but also a monument to Renaissance Italy's long, hard and ultimately unsuccessful struggle towards some kind of social consciousness. Even in the best of times, Florence's poor were treated like dirt; if any enlightened soul had been so bold as to propose even a modern conservative 'trickle-down' theory to the Medici and the banking élite, their first thought would have been how to stop the leaks. Babies, at least, were treated a little better. The Spedale degli Innocenti was the first hospital for foundlings in Italy and the world, and still serves as an orphanage today, as well as the local nursery school.

The Spedale was Brunelleschi's first completed work and demonstrates his use of geometrical proportions adapted to traditional Tuscan Romanesque architecture. His lovely portico is adorned with the famous blue and white *tondi* of infants in swaddling clothes by Andrea della Robbia, added as an appeal to charity in the 1480s after several children died of malnutrition. Brunelleschi also designed the two beautiful cloisters of the convent; the Chiostro delle Donne, reserved for the hospital's nurses, is especially fine (*located up the ramp on the right at No.13*). Upstairs, the **Museo dello Spedale** (*open 8.30–1.30; closed Wed; adm*) contains a number of detached frescoes from Ognissanti and other churches, among them an unusual series of red and orange prophets by Alessandro Allori; other works include a Madonna and Saints by Piero di Cosimo, a *Madonna and Child* by Luca della Robbia, and the brilliant *Adoration of the Magi* (1488) painted by Domenico Ghirlandaio for the hospital's church, a crowded, colourful composition featuring portraits of members of the Arte della Lana, who funded the Spedale.

The second portico on the piazza was built in 1600 in front of Florence's high society church, **Santissima Annunziata**. Founded in 1250, the church was rebuilt by Michelozzo beginning in 1444 and funded by the Medici, who saw the need for a grander edifice to contain the pilgrims attracted by a miraculous image of the Virgin. As a shelter for the crowds, Michelozzo designed the **Chiostrino dei Voti**, an atrium in front of the church. Most of the Chiostrino's frescoes are by Andrea del Sarto and his students but the most enchanting work is Alesso Baldovinetti's *Nativity* (1462)—unfortunately faded, though you can make out the ghost of a transcendent landscape. Also present are two youthful works: Pontormo's *Visitation* and Rosso Fiorentino's more Mannerist *Assumption*.

The interior is the most gaudy, lush Baroque creation in the city, the only one the Florentines ever spent much money on during the Counter-Reformation. Michelozzo's design includes an unusual polygonal tribune around the sanctuary, derived from antique buildings and entered by way of a triumphal arch designed by Alberti. Directly to the left as you enter is Michelozzo's marble *tempietto*, hung with candles, built to house the miraculous *Annunciation*, painted by a monk with the help of an angel who painted the Virgin's face. Its construction was funded by the Medici, who couldn't resist adding an inscription on the floor that 'The marble alone cost 4000 florins'! The ornate canopy over the *tempietto* was added in the 17th century.

The next two chapels on the left side (*the first under restoration*) contain frescoes by Andrea del Castagno, painted in the 1450s but whitewashed over by the Church when it read Vasari's phoney story that Castagno murdered his fellow painter Domenico Veneziano—a difficult feat, since Veneziano outlived his supposed murderer by several years. Rediscovered in 1864, Castagno's fresco of *St Julian and the Saviour* in the first chapel has some strange Baroque bedfellows by Giambattista Foggini; the next chapel contains his highly unusual *Holy Trinity with St Jerome*. The right aisle's fifth chapel contains a fine example of an early Renaissance tomb, that of the obscure Orlando de' Medici by Bernardo Rossellino. The neighbouring chapel in the transept contains a painted crucifix by Baldovinetti, while the next one has a *Pietà*, the funerary monument of Cosimo I's court sculptor and Cellini's arch-rival Baccio Bandinelli; in this *Pietà* he put his own features on Nicodemus, as Michelangelo did in the *Pietà* in the Museo del Duomo. Bandinelli's most lasting contribution (or piece of mischief) was his establishment of the first 'Accademia' of art in 1531, which eventually did away with the old artist-pupil relationship in favour of the more impersonal approach of the art school.

Nine semicircular chapels radiate from the tribune. The one at the rear contains the sarcophagus of Giambologna, a far more successful follower of Michelangelo; his pupil Pietro Tacca is buried with him, in this chapel designed by Giambologna before his death. The next chapel to the left contains a *Resurrection* by Bronzino, one of his finest religious paintings. On the left side of Alberti's triumphal arch, under a statue of St Peter, is the grave of Andrea del Sarto; next to it is the tomb of bishop Angelo Marzi Medici (1546), one of Florence's loudest Counter-Reformation blasts.

A door from the left transept leads into the **Chiostro dei Morti**, most notable for Andrea del Sarto's highly original fresco, the *Madonna del Sacco* (1525), named after the sacks of grain on which St Joseph leans. The **Cappella di San Luca**, located off the cloister (*usually closed, ask the priest*) belongs to Florence's Academy of Design and contains the graves of Cellini, Pontormo, Franciabigio and other artists.

The Other Side of Florence

Alla Vecchia Bettola

Something changes once you cross the Ponte Vecchio. A different Florence reveals itself: greener, quieter, and less burdened with traffic and tourists. The Oltrarno is not a large district. A chain of hills squeezes it against the river, and their summits afford some of the best views over the city. This is a not-so-lazy way to spend a day away from the feverish streets and piazzas of the city centre, one that allows you to see one of Florence's finest churches and a remarkable cycle of frescoes. Lunch is in one of the city's most unexpected restaurants, where you'll find excellent versions of traditional Florentine *trattoria* dishes: bread-based soups such as *ribollita* and *pappa al pomodoro*, offal dishes like tripe and calves' foot, along with rabbit, sausage and salt cod.

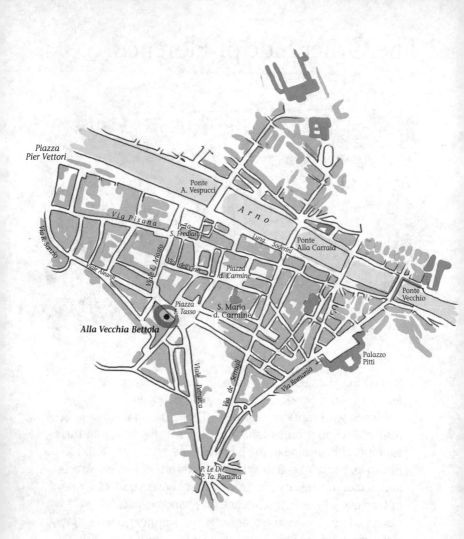

getting there

From Santa Maria del Carmine walk west along Via dell'Orto, then left down Viale Ariosto to Piazza Torquato Tasso. Alla Vecchia Bettola is the small, unassuming-looking place on the opposite side of busy Viale Petrarca.

Alla Vecchia Bettola

Viale Ariosto 32/34R, Florence, © (055) 224158. Closed Sun & Mon, hols two weeks in August. L50,000, no credit cards.

Just a few minutes' walk from Santa Maria del Carmine, yet virtually always devoid of tourists, Alla Vecchia Bettola is understandably one of the favourite restaurants of cookery writer Valentina Harris. With its ceramic tiled walls, high marble-topped tables and wooden benches and stools, it looks like one of those old-fashioned Italian grocery and wine shops, where you could sample as well as buy the produce. Adding to the illusion are the terracotta flasks, huge bunches of garlic, and the lavish display of *funghi porcini*, salamis, hams and cheeses on the counter.

When you arrive you are courteously shown to a table (you may have to share with a solitary diner or a couple of lunching office workers) which is rapidly laid with rough paper place mats. If you don't want the house red or white, which comes in big flasks (you pay for what you drink) the Petrograno Chardonnay is good, light and summery. The menu changes daily, but there are usually a number of old favourites. There's no written menu, but the waiters are genuine food enthusiasts, and happy to explain what everything is. There is also a fascinating free booklet of recipes.

Antipasti are usually a selection of fine salamis and cured meats, though there may be other things on offer, such as *panzanella*, a hearty Tuscan salad made with bread soaked in water for an hour, then mixed with chopped onions, fresh tomatoes, lots of basil, and slices of cucumber, dressed with wine vinegar and olive oil.

As for *primi*, look out for *tagliolini con funghi porcini*, the glistening golden tagliolini cooked perfectly *al dente*, entangling pungent slivers of *porcini* mushrooms. Other regular dishes include home-made pasta served with *sugo finto*, literally fake sauce, so-called because one is supposed not to be able to tell there is no meat in it. It's delicious anyway, a slow-cooked combination of celery, onion, parsley, basil, carrots and tomatoes, served with grated *cacio* cheese. Another filling Tuscan standard is *tortelli di patate*, pasta stuffed with a puree of potatoes, butter, egg, grated cheese and nutmeg, and served with either a tomato or meat sauce.

Whatever you do, don't fail to try Vecchia Bettola's *carpaccio*—definitely among the best in Tuscany—with the utterly tender, juicy and flavoursome taste of the very best steak. Scattered over it is a pile of bitter, peppery roughly shredded rocket and slivers of grainy parmesan cheese. Another speciality is *baccalà* (salt cod) which might be boiled with chickpeas, or stewed with garlic and tomato. Other dishes to look out for include *salsicce con fagioli* (sausages with white beans), *trippa e zampa alla fiorentina* (tripe and calves' feet casseroled with

white wine and tomatoes) and stuffed rabbit. There are also lots of excellent vegetable dishes: *fiori di zucca fritti* (fried courgette flowers), *carciofi fritti* (fried artichokes) and vegetable *frittata* (a baked omelette).

Desserts are simple, but no less delicious for that: the *biscottini* which come with a perky *vin santo* are studded with almonds and hazelnuts and spiked with lemon zest, while the ice cream, which comes from Florence's famous Vivoli, is beautifully velvety. They also do an excellent *torta di mele* and a mean *castagnaccio*, a savoury cake of chestnut flour, rosemary and pine-nuts.

Pappa al Pomodoro

Serves 6

2 onions or 3 leeks, finely chopped

4 tablespoons extra virgin olive oil, plus extra to serve

600g/1lb 5oz plum tomatoes, peeled and chopped

1 tablespoon passata, preferably organic

3 large cloves garlic, finely chopped

1 bunch basil, chopped, plus a few whole leaves to garnish

approx 450g/1lb crusty Tuscan bread cut into 2cm/1 inch cubes

salt and pepper

Gently fry the onions or leeks in half the olive oil until soft. Add the toma-
toes and the preserved tomatoes if you have them. In another pan sauté
the garlic, basil and bread cubes in the remaining oil until very slightly
golden. When the onions and leeks are soft and the tomatoes have col-
lapsed, add the bread. Simmer until the mixture is not quite a pap (i.e. the
bread should not totally disintegrate). Season to taste and serve with a
generous drizzle of extra virgin olive oil and a few leaves of fresh basil.
Incidentally, this dish is even better the day afterwards.

touring around

Just south of the Arno across the Ponte Vecchio, the first building of
note you come to is **Santa Felicità**, one of Florence's most ancient
churches, believed to have been founded by the Syrian-Greek traders
who introduced Christianity to the city and established the first
Christian cemetery in the small square in front of the church. Rebuilt
in the 18th century, it has one compelling reason for you to enter, for
here, in the first chapel on the right, is the *ne plus ultra* of Mannerism:
Pontormo's weirdly luminous *Deposition* (1528), painted in jarring
pinks, oranges and blues that cut through the darkness of the little
chapel. The composition itself is unconventional, with an effect that
derives entirely from the use of figures in unusual, exaggerated poses;
there is no sign of a cross, the only background is a single cloud.
Sharing the chapel is Pontormo's *Annunciation* fresco, a less idiosyncratic work, as well as four *tondi* of the Evangelists in the cupola,
partly the work of Pontormo's pupil and adopted son, Bronzino.

Take a right on Via di Santo Spirito, then the first left on to **Piazza
Santo Spirito**, the centre of the **Oltrarno**. This is a world away from
the city centre, a neighbourly place with a few market stalls in the
morning under the plane trees as well as a quiet café or two. In the
evening it changes face and the bars fill with people, who meet and
chat in the piazza and on the church steps until the early hours. On
one side, a plain 18th-century façade hides Brunelleschi's last and perhaps greatest church. He designed **Santo Spirito** in 1440 and lived to
see only one column erected, but subsequent architects were faithful
to his elegant plan for the interior. This is done in the architect's
favourite pale grey and *pietra serena* articulation, a rhythmic forest of

columns with semicircular chapels gracefully recessed into the transepts and the three arms of the crossing. The effect is somewhat spoiled by the ornate 17th-century *baldacchino*, which sits in this enchanted garden of architecture like a 19th-century bandstand.

The art in the chapels is meagre, as most of the good paintings were sold off. The best include Filippino Lippi's beautiful *Madonna and Saints* in the right transept and Verrocchio's jewel-like *St Monica and Nuns* in the opposite transept, an unusual composition and certainly one of the blackest paintings of the Renaissance, pervaded with a dusky, mysterious quality; Verrocchio, who taught both Leonardo and Botticelli, was a Hermetic alchemist on the side. The fine marble altarpiece and decoration in a nearby chapel is by Sansovino; the elaborate barrel-vaulted vestibule and octagonal sacristy, entered from the left aisle, are by Giuliano da Sangallo, inspired by Brunelleschi.

To the left of the church, in the refectory of the vanished 14th-century convent (*open 8–12, closed Mon; adm*), are the scanty remains of a *Last Supper* and a well-preserved, highly dramatic *Crucifixion* by Andrea Orcagna, in which Christ is seen alone against an enormous dark sky, with humanity ranged below and angels like white swallows swirling around in a cosmic whirlwind. The refectory also contains an interesting collection of Romanesque odds and ends, including 13th-century stone sea-lions from Naples.

There is little to say about the surroundings, the piazza, the rough stone façade, or the interior of the Oltrarno's other great church, **Santa Maria del Carmine** (*open 10–4.30 and 1–4.30 Sun, closed Tues; adm*), which burned in 1771 and was reconstructed shortly after. Miraculously, the **Brancacci Chapel**, one of the landmarks in Florentine art, survived both the flames and attempts by the authorities to replace it with something more fashionable. Three artists worked on the Brancacci's frescoes: Masolino, who began them in 1425, and who designed the cycle, his pupil Masaccio, who worked on them alone for a year before following his master to Rome, where he died at the age of 27, and Filippino Lippi, who finished them 50 years later. Filippino took care to imitate Masaccio as closely as possible, and the frescoes have an appearance of stylistic unity. Between 1981 and 1988 they were subject to one of Italy's most publicized restorations, cleansed of 550 years of dirt and overpainting, enabling us to see what so thrilled the painters of the Renaissance. Masaccio in his day was a revolution and a revelation in his solid, convincing naturalism; his figures stand in space, without any fussy ornamentation or Gothic grace, very much inspired by Donatello's sculptures. Masaccio conveyed emotion with broad, quick brush- strokes and with his use of light, most obvious in his almost Impressionistic scene of the *Expulsion of Adam and Eve*, one of the most memorable and harrowing images created in the Renaissance. In the *Tribute Money*, the young artist displays his mastery of Brunelleschian artificial perspective and light effects. The three episodes in the fresco show an official demanding tribute from the city, St Peter fetching it, on Christ's direction, from the mouth of a fish, and lastly, his handing over of the money to the official. Other works by 'Shabby Tom' include *St Peter Baptizing* on the upper register, and *St Peter Healing with his Shadow* and *St Peter Enthroned and Resurrecting the Son of the King of Antioch*, the right half of which was finished by Filippino Lippi. The more elegant and unearthly Masolino is responsible for the remainder, except for the lower register's *Release of St Peter from Prison*, *St Peter Crucified* and *St Paul Visiting St Peter in Prison*, all by Filippino Lippi, based on Masaccio's sketches.

Don't worry if you're by now befuddled by fantastic frescoes and forests of columns. From Santa Maria it's a brief walk to **Piazza Torquato Tasso** where you'll find Alla Vecchia Bettola.

For a quiet walk after lunch, you could well go for a stroll in the **Boboli Gardens** which stretch back invitingly from the Pitti Palace. Originally laid out by Buontalenti, the Boboli reigns as queen of all formal Tuscan gardens, the most elaborate and theatrical, a Mannerist-Baroque co-production of Nature and artifice laid out over a steep hill, full of shady nooks and pretty walks. The park is guarded by a platoon of statuary, many of them Roman works, while others are absurd Mannerist pieces like Cosimo I's court dwarf posing as a chubby Bacchus astride a turtle (ner the left-hand entrance, next to Vasari's Corridor). Other delights in the park include the remarkable Grotta di Buontalenti, one of the architect's most imaginative works, anticipating Gaudì with his dripping stone from wwhich fantastic limestone animals struggle to emerge; and the Amphitheatre, designed like a small Roman circus to hold Medici court spectacles.

A Rustic Feast in Refined Fiesole

Florence liked to look on itself as the daughter of Rome, and in its fractious heyday explained its quarrelsome nature by the fact that its population from the beginning was of mixed race, of Romans and 'that ungrateful and malignant people who of old came down from Fiesole', according to Dante. First settled in the 2nd millennium BC, it became the most important Etruscan city in the region. The city's relationship with Rome was rocky, but because of its lofty position it was difficult to capture, so the Romans built a camp on the Arno below to cut off its supplies. Eventually Fiesole was taken, and it dwindled as the Roman camp below grew into the city of Florence.

But ever since the days of the *Decameron*, whose storytellers retreated to its garden villas to escape the plague, Fiesole has played the role of Florence's aristocratic suburb; its cool breezes, beautiful landscapes and belvedere views make it the perfect refuge from the torrid Florentine summers. Foreigners have been tramping up and down Fiesole's hill since the days of Shelley. A day trip has become an obligatory part of a stay in Florence, and although Fiesole has proudly retained its status as an independent *comune*, you can make the 20-minute

Badia Fiesolana

trip up on Florence city bus 7 from the station or Piazza San Marco. Inevitably most tourists end up eating in the unexceptional restaurants of the town centre, or paying over the odds for a meal at the luxurious Villa San Michele hotel. A far better alternative is to drive 2km to the village of Maiano, to eat hearty food in a traditional restaurant much loved by locals.

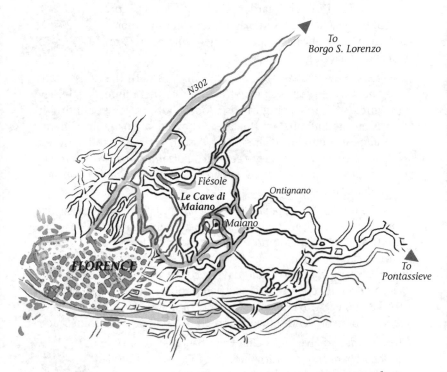

getting there

As you descend the hill from Fiesole heading towards Florence, drive past the Villa San Michele hotel, then look out for a sign to Maiano. The narrow road, bordered by a high wall leads straight to the village. Once in Maiano, a sign directs you left to the restaurant, a stone building which stands on the roadside.

Le Cave di Maiano

Via delle Cave 16, Maiano, nr Fiesole, ☏ (055) 59133, ✉ (055) 599504.
Closed Mon lunch. L45,000 excluding wine, all credit cards.

This is an animated, rustic little place where those in the know come to eat good, honest home cooking on a tremendous leafy terrace with magnficent views over a steep green valley. To get in, you pass first through a larder-lobby with a huge anti-quated fridge and, in season, baskets of wild mushrooms, and then through a cramped kitchen where chefs are ferociously hacking huge steaks.

Waiters show you swiftly to a table, and, as both the house white and red are great, you may as well order them immediately. The white is the refreshing Fattoria Montellori, which you'll find in various restaurants in the area, the red a quaffable Chianti. *Antipasti* are traditional: *crostini*, Tuscan *prosciutto*, and, best, the *misto caldo*, with chewy deep-fried *polenta* topped with garlicky *porcini*, and nicely toasted, generously topped *crostini di pomodoro* and *pâté di fegato*.

Primi are homely, with *pappa al pomodoro* and *riso allo spazzacamino* flying the Tuscan flag. The former is a nice, comforting bready-tomato pap, the latter an uncompromisingly rustic dish you won't find in many restaurants, consisting of rice, beans and *cavolo nero* (black cab-bage). It's best saved for a cold day, laced with plenty of olive oil and black pepper. If you don't feel like going totally rustic, have the *ravioli rosé*, golden eggy ravioli stuffed with ricotta and spinach which actu-ally taste of ricotta and spinach, dressed in a tomato and cream sauce.

The *secondi* also give you a chance to try peasant food, with the *fagottini di cavolo alla contadina*, cabbage leaves rolled around a pink grainy sausage and covered with mush-rooms. An acquired taste. If you're not feeling adventurous, try the superb *piccione arrosto*, grilled pigeon, the *pollastro al mattone*, grilled spatchcocked chicken, or, of course, a *bistecca alla fiorentina*. With any of these you can order a green salad.

Desserts are wheeled in on a trolley–look out for fresh fig flan–or just opt for *biscotti* and *vin santo*.

Cantuccini

Although originating in Prato, cantucci *or* cantuccini *are now served in restaurants all over Tuscany. They are twice-cooked biscuits usually served with a glass of vin santo for dipping.*

300g/11oz plain flour
1¼ teaspoons baking powder
pinch of salt
175g/6oz caster sugar
2 whole eggs plus 2 egg yolks
125g/4½oz almonds, coarsely chopped
1 tablespoon milk

Butter and lightly flour a baking sheet. Sift the flour, baking powder and salt into a bowl, add the sugar, whole eggs and one of the egg yolks and mix to a soft dough. Stir in the almonds. Divide the dough into 2 portions and form each into a long sausage, about 2.5cm/1 inch in diameter and 30 cm/12 inches long. Mix together the milk and remaining egg yolk and use to brush the dough. Bake in an oven preheated to 180°C/350°F (gas mark 4) until golden (about 20 minutes).

While still soft, cut the rolls into diagonal slices about 1cm/½ inch thick. Separate the slices and arrange on the baking sheet so that they are not touching. Return to the oven and bake for about 10 minutes, until golden brown and crisp. Cool on a wire rack and store in an airtight tin.

---

touring around

The long, sloping stage of **Piazza Mino** is Fiesole's centre, with the bus stop, the local tourist office, the cafés, and the **Palazzo Pretorio**, its *loggia* and façade emblazoned with coats-of-arms. The square is named after a favourite son, the quattrocento sculptor Mino da Fiesole, whom Ruskin preferred to all others. An example of his work may be seen in the Duomo, whose plain façade dominates the north side of the piazza. Built in 1028, it was the only building spared by the vindictive Florentines in 1125. It was subsequently enlarged and given a scouring 19th-century restoration, leaving the tall, crenellated campanile as its sole distinguishing feature. Still, the interior has an austere charm, with a raised choir over the crypt similar to San Miniato. Up the steps to the right are two beautiful works by Mino da Fiesole: the *Tomb of Bishop Leonardo Salutati* and an altar front. The main altarpiece in the choir, of the *Madonna and Saints*, is by Lorenzo di Bicci, from 1440. Note the two saints frescoed on the columns; it was a north Italian custom to paint holy people as if they were members of the congregation. The crypt, holding the remains of Fiesole's patron, St Romulus, is supported by ancient columns bearing doves, spirals and other early Christian symbols.

Behind the cathedral, on Via Dupré, the **Bandini Museum** (*open 10–7 daily, exc Tues; in winter 10–6; adm*) contains more sacred works, including numerous della Robbia terracottas, and some good trecento paintings by Lorenzo Monaco, Neri di Bicci and Taddeo Gaddi.

Behind the cathedral and museum is the entrance to what remains of *Faesulae*. Because Fiesole avoided trouble in the Dark Ages, its Roman monuments have survived in much better shape than those of Florence; although hardly spectacular, the ruins are charmingly set amid olive groves and cypresses. The small Roman theatre has survived well enough to host plays and concerts in the summer; Fiesole would like to remind you that in the ancient times it had the theatre and plays while Florence had the amphitheatre and wild beast shows. Close by are the rather confusing remains of two superimposed temples, the baths, and an impressive stretch of Etruscan walls (best seen from Via delle Mure Etrusche) that proved their worth against Hannibal's siege. The Archaeology Museum (*open 9–7 summer; 9–6 winter, closed Tues; adm*) is housed in a small 20th-century Ionic temple, displaying some very early small bronze figurines with flapper wing arms, Etruscan funerary urns and *stelae*, including the interesting 'stele Fiesolana' with a banquet scene.

From Piazza Mino, **Via S. Francesco** ascends steeply (at first) to the hill that served as the Etruscan and Roman acropolis. Halfway up is a terrace with extraordinary views of Florence and the Arno sprawl, with a monument to the three *carabinieri* who gave themselves up to be shot by the Nazis in 1944 to prevent them from taking civilian reprisals. The church nearby, the **Basilica di Sant'Alessandro**, was constructed over an Etruscan/Roman temple in the 6th century, re-using its lovely *cipollino* (onion marble) columns and Ionic capitals, one still inscribed with an invocation to Venus. At the top of the hill, square on the ancient acropolis, stands the **monastery of San Francesco**, its church containing a famous early cinquecento *Annunciation* by Raffaellino del Garbo and an *Immaculate Conception* by Piero di Cosimo. A grab-bag of odds and ends collected from the four corners of the world, especially Egypt and China, is displayed in the quaint **Franciscan Missionary Museum** (*open 10–12 and 3–6 summer; 10–12 and 3–5 winter*) in the cloister; it also has an Etruscan collection.

There are much longer walks along the hill behind the Palazzo Pretorio. The panoramic Via Belvedere leads back to Via Adriano Mari, and in a couple of kilometres to the bucolic **Montecéceri**, a wooded park where Leonardo da Vinci performed his flight experiments, and where Florentine architects once quarried their dark *pietra serena* from quarries now abandoned but open for exploration. In Borgunto, as this part of Fiesole is called, there are two 3rd-century BC **Etruscan tombs** on Via Bargellino; east of Borgunto scenic Via Francesco Ferrucci and Via di Vincigliata pass by Fiesole's castles, the **Castel di Poggio**, site of summer concerts, and the **Castel di Vincigliata**, dating back to 1031, while further down is American critic Bernard Berenson's famous **Villa I Tatti**, which he left, along with a distinguished collection of Florentine art, to Harvard University as the Centre of Italian Renaissance Studies. The road continues down towards Ponte a Mensola and Settignano, with buses back to Florence.

Located between Fiesole and Florence, **San Domenico di Fiesole** is a pleasant walk down from Fiesole by way of Via Vecchia Fiesolana, the steep and narrow old road that passes, on the left, the **Villa Medici**, built by Michelozzo for Cosimo il Vecchio; in its lovely garden on the hillside, Lorenzo and his friends of the Platonic Academy would come to get away from the world; it was also the lucky Iris Origo's childhood home. San Domenico, at the bottom of the lane, is the church and convent where Fra Angelico first entered his monkish world. The 15th-century church of San Domenico contains his lovely *Madonna with Angels and Saints*, in the first chapel on the left, as well as a photograph of his *Coronation of the Virgin*, which the French snapped up in 1809 and sent to the Louvre. Across the nave there's a *Crucifixion* by the school of Botticelli, an unusual composition of verticals highlighted by the cypresses in the background. In the chapterhouse of the monastery (*ring the bell at No.4*) Fra' Angelico left a fine fresco of the *Crucifixion* and a *Madonna and Child*, which is shown with its synopia, before moving down to Florence and San Marco.

The lane in front of San Domenico leads down in five minutes to the **Badia Fiesolana** (*open Sun am only*), the ancient cathedral of Fiesole, built in the 9th century by Fiesole's bishop, an Irishman named Donatus, with a fine view over the rolling countryside and Florence in the background. Though later enlarged, perhaps by Brunelleschi, it has preserved the elegant façade of the older church, a charming example of the geometric green and white marble inlay decoration that characterizes Tuscan Romanesque churches. The interior is adorned with *pietra serena* very much in the style of Brunelleschi. The convent buildings next door are now the home of the European University Institute.

A Majestic and Imperious Wine

*From good Chianti, an aged wine, majestic and
imperious, that passes through my heart and chases
away without trouble every worry and grief ...*

Francesco Redi, *Bacchus in Tuscany*

In the 17th century, naturalist and poet Francesco
Redi was the first to note the virtues of 'Florentine
red' from Chianti. The name apparently derives from an
Etruscan family named Clanti; geographically it refers,
roughly, to the hilly region between Florence and Siena, bordered by the Florence–Siena Superstrada del Palio and the A1
from Florence to Arezzo. The part within Siena province is
known as Chianti Storico or Chianti Geografico, once the territories of the Lega del Chianti, a consortium of barons formed
in 1385, who adopted a black cockerel as their emblem.

But Chianti is an oenological name as well as a geographical
one, and as such first became official in 1716, when Grand
Duke Cosimo III defined which parts of Tuscany could call
their vintage Chianti, in effect making wine history—it was
the first time that a wine had had its production area delim-
ited. The Lorraine grand dukes promoted advances in
winemaking techniques and Chianti export. Yet the Chianti as
we know it was largely the creation of one man—the 'Iron
Baron', Bettino Ricasoli, briefly the second prime minister of
unified Italy. The baron was very wealthy but not very good-
looking, and Luigi Barzini, in *The Italians*, recounts how
jealous he became when a young man asked his new bride to
dance at a ball in Florence. Ricasoli at once ordered her into
their carriage and gave the driver the address of the ancient
family seat at Brolio in the Monti del Chianti—an isolated
castle that the poor woman rarely left ever after. To pass the
time the baron began to experiment with different vines and

processes, eventually hitting on a mix of red Sangiovese and Canaiolo grapes, with a touch of white Malvasia, twice fermented in the old Tuscan manner. At the same time the famous dark green flask was invented, the *strapeso*, with its straw covering woven by the local women. The end product took the Paris Exhibition of 1878 by storm; imitators soon appeared, and in 1924, the boundaries of Chianti Storico were slightly more than doubled to create Chianti Classico. In 1967 Chianti Classico, along with Tuscany's six other Chianti vinicultural zones, was given its *denominazione di origine* status, and production soared, but quality and sales declined. To improve the wine, the Chianti Classico Consortium was upscaled to a DOCG rating to guarantee that all wines bearing the black cockerel would be tested and approved by a panel of judges.

But it was tales of Elizabeth Barrett Browning quaffing Chianti and finding her inspiration in its ruby splendour, as well as the sunny rural elegance of the region, that attracted first the English and Dutch, then the Swiss, Americans, French and Germans. They brought into the region more money than Chianti's mouldering barons and *contessas* had seen since the Renaissance; real property prices shot to the moon. But the presence of so much money has begun to cast a shadow over the heart of this ancient, enchanting region; snobbery and pretensions threaten to poison the pleasurable plonk of yesteryear; limited edition numbered bottles, offered by some vintners, are a bit too much. The old vines, following the contours of the hills, are being pulled out for specialized vines in geometric straight lines. And as any old-timer will tell you, the modern DOCG Chianti Classico sniffed and gurgled by wine professionals isn't anything like the joyous, spontaneous wine that made Chianti famous in the first place.

The following three chapters take you on a journey to the heart of 'Chiantishire'.

Eating off the Land:
the Montagliari Estate

Some 800 farms and estates produce wine in the mere 70,000 hectares in the Chianti Classico zone, and one of the chief pleasures in visiting is trying as many labels as possible—with the different mixtures of grapes, different soils, and different bottling methods, each should be, or at least strives to be, individual. Nor do the estates limit themselves to Chianti; many produce *vin santo*, a white wine called Bianca della Lega, and many reds, as well as Chianti's other speciality, an especially delicate extra-virgin olive oil.

The focus of this day out is the Montagliari estate, which lies on the Chiantigiana 4 kilometres outside Greve. It creates fine wines, *vin santo*, *grappa* and olive oil, brews its own balsamic-style vinegar, and produces a whole range of gastronomic delicacies ranging from herb-infused oils, sauces and pestos to *cantucci* and grape, fig and blackberry conserves. It also has a superb *trattoria*. This is a truly lazy day, spent browsing around Greve and some of the neighbouring vineyards.

montagliari Estate

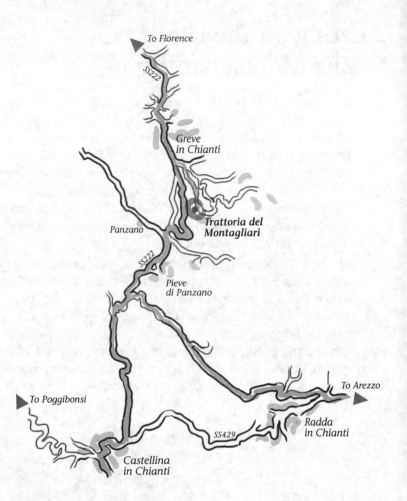

To Florence

SS222

Greve in Chianti

Panzano

Trattoria del Montagliari

SS222

Pieve di Panzano

To Poggibonsi

To Arezzo

Radda in Chianti

SS429

Castellina in Chianti

getting there

Leave Greve on the SS222 heading south towards Panzano. The Montagliari estate is clearly signposted about 4km along the road. It stands on your left, at the foot of the hill that climbs up to Panzano.

Trattoria del Montagliari

Panzano in Chianti, Greve in Chianti, ✆ (055) 852184, 📠 (055) 852014.
Closed Mon, 1 week Aug. L40,000–L60,000.

The Trattoria del Montagliari comes pretty close to the collective dream of the perfect Tuscan *trattoria*. It is set on the Montagliari estate, and in summer you sit on a gorgeous terrace shaded by acacia trees and bordered with wild roses looking out over the Montagliari vineyards to the Val di Greve. In cool weather you eat in the authentically rustic dining room of the mellow stone 18th-century *casa colonica*. Most days, the rotund proprietor Giovanni Capelli is to be found lunching in shirt-sleeves with his family or local businessmen. The food is excellent too, the sort of simple, homely fare that relies absolutely on the excellence of the ingredients—and fortunately there are plenty of great raw materials in the vicinity.

You could start, for example, with a *panzanese di pecorino del Chianti*, an invention of Giovanni, which substitutes the *mozzarella di bufala* of Caprese for *pecorino fresco*, slices of sharp, milky fresh (under 12 days old) *pecorino* served with slices of tomato and torn basil leaves. Alternatively try another local product, *crostini di milza*, rounds of toast spread with a warm, spicy pungent pâté, which is delicious even when you discover that *milza* means spleen. It is made up in Panzano by a classical-music-playing butcher at Da Cecchino (*see* p.88).

In season the *zuppa di funghi porcini* is a must. Other primi worth trying include *penne strascicate al sugo di pecora*, with a scant sauce of succulent minced lamb gently spiked with chilli, clinging to broad tubes of *penne*; or light *gnocchi con pomodoro fresco e basilico* (gnocchi with fresh tomato and basil).

For a *secondo*, local lamb is the thing to go for (although there's good Tuscan duck and Chianina steak as well). *Agnellino al forno*, roast young lamb, is meltingly good, though not for anyone concerned about their animal fat intake; cholesterol-watchers had better go for *cotolette d'agnello alla brace*, lamb cutlets, still pink and juicy, grilled with herbs. As for vegetables, there's usually a tempting choice—look out for locally grown beans (*fagioli*), peppers (*peperonata*) and beetroot greens (*bietola*).

As for the desserts, don't leave without trying the *torta di mele*, an apple pie to beat most, caramelly on the edges, soft, juicy and buttery in the middle, and totally moreish. Pair it up with *vin santo*.

To finish, have a glass of *limoncello*, a thick iced, fiery lemon liqueur which makes lemon vodka seem like lemonade.

Fagioli Cotti nel Fiasco

The traditional way of cooking fagioli (white beans) is to put them in an empty Chianti bottle (with the straw wrapping removed) with some olive oil, herbs and a little water inside and leave them to cook for several hours beside or above the embers of a charcoal fire. Aficionados will tell you that this is the best way to cook beans—the bottle's narrow opening keeps in all the flavours and perfumes. However, Chianti bottles are no longer made of a glass resistant enough, so it is probably best to use a casserole. Cover and cook the beans (if using dried haricot beans, soak them first) on a slow heat for several hours, as described above. Just before serving, add more olive oil and garnish with tuna fish, herrings or anchovies; alternatively you can add more oil, some sage, garlic and chopped tomatoes and reheat the beans until the tomatoes have disintegrated.

---

touring around

Panzano in Chianti, near to the Montagliari estate, is an important agricultural centre. It is a little hilltop village which played an important role in the Florence–Siena squabbles, but retains only part of its medieval castle. Today it is best known for its embroidery, and visited for the **Pieve di San Leolino**, 1km south, with its pretty 16th-century portico on a 12th-century Romanesque structure; inside there's a triptych by Mariotto di Nardo. Foodies, however, will probably prefer to make pilgrimages to Da Cecchino, a small family butcher's which has been running for 200 years, and rigorously maintains traditional standards. The young owner is a classical music fan, so you can listen to Mozart and Verdi while you deliberate over which salami or pâté to buy. Following the sign to Panzano Alta, you'll come to to a shop marked 'Alimentari Forno a Legno'. In the wood oven, a fabulous local sugar-crusted raisin bread is baked, known as *schiacciata panzanesa*. If you have time, drive out of town past the butcher's, along a rough road signposted to **Cennatoio**. After about four slow kilometres you'll come to a crossroads marked on the map as **Il Sodo**. Here there's a small dairy farm, where a Sardinian couple, the Tolus, make their own pecorino cheese every day at 7am and 7pm (*© (055) 854 7056*).

The biggest wine fair in Chianti occurs every September in the medieval townlet of **Greve** (pop. 10,800), a few kilometres north of Panzano, and as such it is looked upon as the capital of Chianti. Located on the banks of the river Greve, it is celebrated for its charming, arcaded, funnel-shaped **Piazza del Mercatale**, with a statue of Verrazzano in its centre. And that's about all—its castle was burned in 1387, and its Franciscan convent converted to a prison in the last century. However, in the parish church of **Santa Croce** there's a triptych by Lorenzo di Bicci and a painting by the 'Master of Greve'.

Unsurprisingly, Greve is awash in wine and food. On Piazza del Mercatale don't miss the flamboyant butcher's shop, Falorni, a 300-year old concern which produces a dazzling array of salamis, cured hams and sausages. Seek out too specialized wine shops like the Bottega del Chianti Classico, Via Cesare Battisti 4, *©* 853 631, and the Enoteca del Chianti Classico, Piazzetta S. Croce 8, *©* 853 297, or the Castello di Querceto just outside town on the Figline Val d'Arno road, *©* 854 9064, a lovely place offering a wide variety of wines, including Sangiovese aged in wooden barriques and olive oil (*tastings with one week's notice*). On the Chiantigiana, near Sant'Eufrosino, Fontodi, Via S. Leonino 87, *©* 852 005, also has wine aged in barriques, Chianti, Bianco della Lega and olive oil (*tastings with one week's notice*).

In a nearby hamlet, **Cintoia**, east of Chiocchio, there is the little church of Santa Maria a Cintoia with a beautiful 15th-century panel attributed to Francesco Granacci.

A kilometre to the west of Greve is the ancient village and castle of **Montefioralle**, where the people of Greve lived in the bad old days. Recently restored, it is an interesting place to poke around in, with its octagonal walls intact, its old tower houses, and two Romanesque churches, **Santo Stefano**, housing early Florentine paintings, and the porticoed **Pieve di San Cresci a Montefioralle**, just outside the walls. A minor road west of Montefioralle passes in a kilometre the ruined

castle of Montefili, built in the 900s as the eastern outpost of one of Chianti's most powerful religious institutions, the Badia a Passignano, a fortified complex of ancient foundation, since converted into a villa. The old abbey church, **San Michele**, can be visited, and contains paintings by Ghirlandaio, Alessandro Allori and Domenico Cresti (better known as Passignano) and a bust of San Giovanni Gualberto, founder of the Vallombrosan Order, who arrived here preaching reform in the mid-11th century. Most of the buildings you see date from the 14th century, with a few remodellings in the 17th and 19th centuries.

Just east of Greve, **Vignamaggio** is the site of a beautiful old villa built by the Gherardini family, the most famous member of whom, Lisa, was born here, and later married Francesco del Giocondo before going on to pose for the world's most famous portrait. In 1992 the villa was used as the setting for Kenneth Branagh's film version of *Much Ado About Nothing*.

A Piazza without a City

A glass of wine on a garden terrace, the olives glinting in the midday sun and geometric vineyards losing their rigid order as they curl into the distance, the cypresses on the hills standing out like dark daggers   the Chianti region is the very image of Tuscany.

In the middle of the region, La Piazza is a minuscule hamlet overlooking the rolling hills of Chianti between Castellina in Chianti and the village of Panzano. It is home to a rather unusual restaurant, run by Giovanni Lecchini, a former engineer, in his family's ancestral home, a mellow stone-built farmhouse.

La Piazza is an easy and pleasant drive from Siena, but it's worth leaving yourself plenty of time so you can drop into wineries en route.

osteria alla Piazza

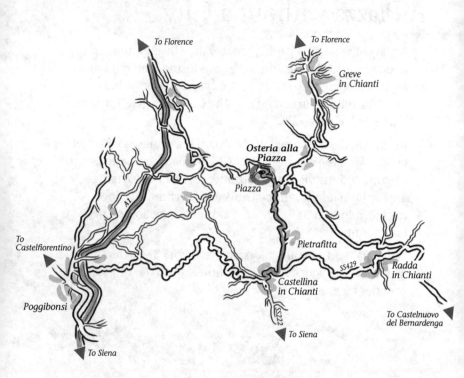

getting there

From Castelllina in Chianti, head north, following signs to Greve in Chianti and Pietrafitta. La Piazza is a hamlet about 5km beyond Pietrafitta. Approaching from Castellina, the turning is clearly signposted to your left. As soon as you enter the hamlet you will see the golden stone-built farmhouse. Directly behind it is a sign marked Fattoria San Giorgio alla Piazza, a farm also owned by the Lecchini family where you can buy wine, oil and honey.

Osteria alla Piazza

La Piazza, Nr Castellina in Chianti, © (0577) 733580. Closed Mon. L60,000, Visa/Mastercard.

When your tastebuds are tired of *crostini toscani*, *funghi porcini* and *bistecca alla fiorentina* (and after a week in Tuscany they will be), make your way to the tiny hamlet of La Piazza. Here, in an old stone farmhouse adorned with roses, you'll find a tranquil restaurant where you can eat imaginative, but never fussy, food on a terrace with magnificent views over the soft wood—and vineyard-cloaked Chianti hills.

The Osteria alla Piazza was founded in 1989 by Giovanni Lecchini, then an engineer, in his old family house. Though it's rather a refined place, it is far from stuffy, and service is amiable and attentive. The menu is nicely balanced between traditional and more original dishes, and there are around a dozen specials every day. The wine-list is interesting, with lots of lesser-known Chiantis as well as the big names. Waiters will help you choose wines to go with food you have ordered. For lighter dishes, the young, lively Chianti Classico Montesassi 91 is a good choice,

Antipasti, depending on the day and season, can range from *crostine di polpo*, a giant *crostino* topped with octopus in a creamy sauce, to an excellent *bruschetta con pomodoro*, the *bruschetta* soaked in a fruity olive oil and piled high with sweet tomatoes and torn basil, far more tangy and sprightly than the supermarket variety we get in the UK.

Although the *primi* include hearty Tuscan staples like *zuppa di funghi* and *pappardelle al sugo di cinghiale*, it's worth trying one of the more original dishes. There's *girasole ai quattro sapori* (a single giant tortelloni stuffed with courgettes, cauliflower, aubergine and parsley); the unusual *spaghetti piccanti con pomodoro e rucola* (spaghetti in a fiery tomato sauce topped with a pile of cubed fresh tomato and peppery rocket); or *farfalle con pesto e pomodoro fresco* (butterfly-shaped pasta cloaked in aromatic pesto, with fresh tomato and torn basil on top).

As for *secondi*, La Piazza specialises in *tagliata*, thin strips of steak served with, say, *funghi porcini* or asparagus. It tends to be very salty, so it's advisable to ask to have yours done with no or little salt. Other dishes range from *bistecca alla fiorentina* to the delicate *spigola in salsa di lattuga* (sea bass cooked with lettuce).

There are some good salads as well—including a tasty *pecorino* and rocket combination.

Desserts vary daily—look out for *torta di mele*, *torta di ricotta* and *tiramisu*. The house *biscottini*, served with *vin santo*, are best avoided unless you're feeling nostalgic for a chocolate and cornflake crispy.

Spaghetti Piccanti con Pomodoro e Rucola

Serves 4

2 tablespoons extra virgin olive oil, plus extra to serve
pinch of dried chilli flakes
2 cloves garlic, crushed
450g/1lb tomatoes, peeled, seeded and chopped
400g/14oz spaghetti
1 bunch basil, roughly torn
1 bunch rocket, chopped
salt and pepper

This sauce cooks in approximately the same time it takes to cook the spaghetti. Heat the oil in a pan, add the chilli and garlic and cook gently for a moment, then add three quarters of the tomatoes. Simmer for 10 minutes. Meanwhile, cook the spaghetti in a large pan of boiling water until al dente. Drain and add to the sauce with the basil and a generous drizzle of extra virgin olive oil. Season to taste and stir well. Divide between 4 serving plates and top with a pile of rocket and the rest of the chopped (raw) tomatoes.

touring around

Leaving Siena and heading north along the SS222 or Chiantigiana towards La Piazza, your first stop could be at **Quercegrossa**, birthplace of the great quattrocento sculptor Jacopo della Quercia. A byroad forks northeast for **Vagliagli**, site of the medieval Fattoria della Aiola, © (0577) 322 615, with wines, *grappa*, olive oil, honey and vinegar.

Continuing along the Chiantigiana you'll come to the **Castello di Campalli** near **Fonterutoli**, an ancient hamlet south on the Chiantigiana. In the 13th century Florence and Siena often met here trying to work out peace settlements, none of which endured very long. Peace, however, is the rule at the prestigious Fattoria di Fonterutoli, in the family since 1435, © (0577) 740 309, producing wine in traditional oaken casks, Chianti, Bianco della Lega, and other wines, honey, products made from lavender, and an *extra-vergine* that many consider Tuscany's finest.

Further north, **Castellina in Chianti** is one of Chianti's most charming hilltop villages, Castellina (pop. 2700) was fortified by Florence as an outpost against Siena, and for centuries its fortunes depended on who was momentarily on top in their bitter, stupid, endless war. Most grievous to the Florentines was its loss to a combined Sienese-Aragonese siege in 1478, though after the fall of Siena itself in 1555 both cities lost interest in Castellina, and today it looks much as it did in the quattrocento: the old circuit of walls is almost intact, complete with houses built into and on top of them; the **Rocca**, or fortress, in the centre, its mighty donjon now home of the mayor; and the covered walkway, or **Via delle Volte**, part of the 15th-century defensive works. Less historic but just as worth visiting is the Bottega del Vino Gallo Nero, Via della Rocca 10, with a vast assortment of wines and olive oils. A kilometre from the centre, you can explore the **Ipogeo Etrusco di Montecalvario**, a 6th-century BC Etruscan tomb that has recently been restored. West of Castellina on S429, **Granaio** is synonymous with one of Chianti's most renowned wineries, the Melini Wine House, established in 1705 and one of the big innovators in Chianti technology.

Supermiranda

La Villa Miranda

East of Castellina in Chianti
lies the steeper, more rugged region of the Monti del Chianti.
One of the higher hills supports the ancient capital of the Lega
del Chianti (*see* p.83), Radda in Chianti (pop. 1650) at the
entrance to which, in the area known as Villa, you'll find Villa
Miranda. This is another great day out in Chianti, with lots of
castles, abbeys and vineyards to be seen. But be warned, the
restaurant at Villa Miranda is the sort of place where a whole
afternoon can slip away. If it does, and if after supping a bottle
of the estate-produced Supermiranda, you're in no fit state to
drive, there are very reasonably priced rooms to be had, with
swimming pools where you can work off the lunch damage.

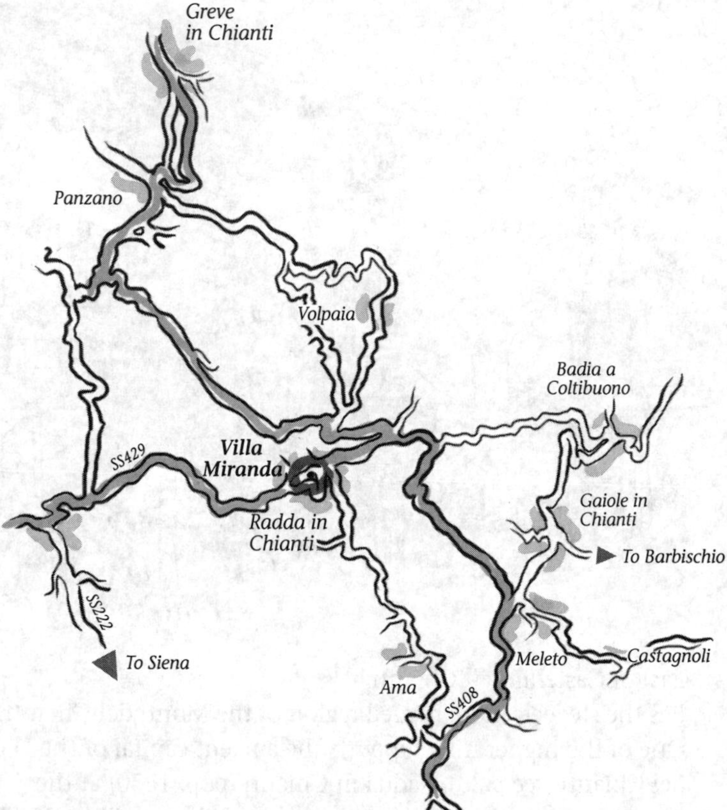
Greve
in Chianti
Panzano
Volpaia
Badia a
Coltibuono
Villa
Miranda
SS429
Radda in
Chianti
Gaiole in
Chianti
To Barbischio
SS222
To Siena
Meleto
Castagnoli
Ama
SS408
To Siena

getting there

A nice easy place to find. Heading towards Radda from Greve and Panzano, Villa Miranda is the stone-built inn on the right which you come across as soon as you enter Radda.

Villa Miranda

Località Villa, Radda in Chianti, ℗ (0577) 738021, ✆ (0577) 738668.
L50,000 (more with a bistecca alla fiorentina*), Visa.*

Donna Miranda is a great big-hearted Tuscan *mamma* who welcomes everyone to her restaurant like long-lost relatives. Dressed in overalls and pinny, with her hair scraped back into a huge headscarf, she buzzes from kitchen to reception to dining room, then collapses a while at a long table in the hall, overseeing bills and catching up on accounts while she keeps an eye on what's going on. This is a chaotic family affair, so don't come if you're in a hurry, and don't be surprised to be sharing the beamed dining room with a convention of gourmandizing bishops. Service is usually by either Miranda's earnest daughter, a doctor in Siena, or a moody teenage nephew. Meanwhile, an old lady, so frail she dare not cross the road, dutifully gets on with the preparations in a picturesque kitchen dominated by a huge wood fire.

Villa Miranda is an old stone house on the road to Radda, overlooking a smallish vineyard. There's a small courtyard outside, but as the road runs close it is far pleasanter to eat within the cool stone walls of the

La villa miranda

dining room. There is a good-value set menu (with a choice of certain *primi* and *secondi*, along with *contorno* and fruit) for L25,000, but the food—good honest Tuscan fare—is so delicious, you may want to indulge as well in an *antipasto* and dessert.

The house wine comes from the vineyard a couple of metres from your table, and the white is perfect for a summer lunch: lively, characterful, lemony, and only too easy to drink. The *bruschetta al pomodoro* here is marvellous, the garlic-rubbed toasted bread piled high with sweet tomatoes collapsing with ripeness, and plenty of basil. Also good are the *crostini neri e verdi*, one with rough-textured chicken liver pâté and the other with a piquant creamy pale green blend of garlic and parsley, and, when figs are in season a succulent *prosciutto e fichi*.

Miranda's *zuppa di farro* is gorgeous—a rich, russety, meaty broth with a breath of chilli, and lots of moist chewy spelt. The *ribollita* can be a bit salty but the *ravioli al burro e salvia* or *pappardelle alla lepre* (hare) are very good. That marvellous wood-fired range in the kitchen makes for an unforgettable *bistecca alla fiorentina*, 18 inches across, 2 inches thick, charred, woodsmoky and herby on the outside, red, juicy and intensely flavourful inside (if you're queasy about raw beef, ask to have it *ben cotta*). Accompany it with a bottle of Supermiranda—a

memorable red surreally reminiscent of an incense-suffused church interior—a basket of crusty bread, and a bowl of *fagioli*, fresh pale green broad beans which you have drizzled with olive oil.

As for dessert, have an ice cream, *torta di mele* or *torta di nocciole* by all means, but be sure to save room for the unputdownable sugar-crusted almond *biscotti*, among the best in Tuscany—and a glass of sweet tangy home-produced *vin santo* to dunk them in. Then, after an *espresso* and *digestivo*, there's really only one thing to do. Book one of Miranda's rooms for the night (the nicest are in converted stone outhouses up in the vineyard), stagger into bed, then have a swim in the pool and an evening stroll to work up an appetite for dinner.

Zuppa di Farro

Serves 6

450g/1lb borlotti beans (or 2x400g/14oz tins of beans)
400g/14oz spelt (farro) (buy this in Tuscany)
3 tablespoons extra virgin olive oil
½ onion, chopped
2 cloves garlic, chopped
1 sprig rosemary, chopped
300g/11oz plum tomatoes, peeled and chopped
pinch of fennel seeds
2 litres/3½ pints chicken or light stock
salt and pepper

Soak the beans and spelt in water overnight in separate bowls (if you are using canned beans, there is no need to soak and precook them). The next day, drain the beans, then cover with fresh water and boil until tender. Drain the beans and purée half of them in a blender. Heat the oil in a large saucepan, add the onion, garlic and rosemary and cook gently until the onion is soft and translucent. Add the drained spelt, plus the puréed and whole beans, tomatoes, fennel seeds and stock, and bring slowly to the boil. Simmer gently for around 4 hours. Season to taste and serve.

touring around

The streets of **Radda in Chianti** have kept their medieval plan, radiating from the central piazza and its stately Palazzo Comunale, encrusted with coats-of-arms and a 15th-century fresco in the atrium of the Madonna, St John the Baptist and St Christopher. Just outside the town is a pretty porticoed Franciscan church, called the Monastero, dating from the 15th century. There are two resolutely medieval villages nearby: **Ama**, with its castle, 8km to the south, near the attractive Romanesque church of San Giusto; and **Volpaia**, 7km to the north, with another ancient castle and walls, and an unexpected 'Brunelleschian' church, called La Commenda, in a doll-sized piazza.

Some day, on a trip to one of the fancier Italian food shops, you may pause near the section devoted to condiments and wonder at the beautiful display of bottles of unusually dark whiskies and wines, with corks and posh, elegant labels—why, some is even DOC, though much of it is far more costly than the usual DOC vintages. A closer look reveals these precious bottles are full of nothing but olive oil. Admittedly *olio extra vergine di oliva* from Tuscany and Umbria makes a fine salad dressing—according to those in the know, the oil of the Chianti brooks few rivals, Italian or otherwise. Its delicate, fruity fragrance derives from the excellent quality of the ripe olive and the low acidity extracted from the fruit without any refinements. The finest oil, Extra Virgin, must have less than 1 per cent acidity (the best has 0.5 per cent acidity). Other designations are Soprafino Virgin, Fine Virgin, and Virgin (each may have up to 4 per cent acidity) in descending order of quality. And as any Italian will tell you, it's good for you—and it had better be, because Tuscan chefs put it in nearly every dish, as they have for centuries. Near Radda, the Fattoria Vigna Vecchia, ✆ 738 090, offers Chianti, *grappa*, *vin santo*, olive oil and tastings (*three days' notice*).

Gaiole, 10km east of Radda, is reached by way of the ancient **Badia a Coltibuono**, one of the gems of Chianti, a singular place set among centuries-old trees and gardens. The abbey is believed to have been founded in 770, but passed over to the Vallombrosan Order in the 12th century. The Romanesque church of San Lorenzo dates from 1049, while the monastery was converted into a splendid villa, owned in the 19th century by the Poniatowski, one of Poland's greatest noble families, and now occupied by a wine estate (P. Stucchi Prinetti, ✆ (0577) 749 498) and restaurant.

Gaiole in Chianti (pop. 4780) was an ancient market town and these days is basically a modern one; the Agricoltori Chianti Geografico, Via Mulinaccio 10, ✆ (0577) 749 489, is the headquarters of a local cooperative where you can purchase Chianti, Vernaccia di San Gimignano, *vin santo* and olive oil; the Enoteca Montagnani, Via B. Bandinelli 9, specializes in Chianti Classico.

Beside wine-tasting, Gaiole has little to offer, but serves as a starting point for visiting the impressive castles in this strategic area between the Arno and Siena. Just to the west are the walls and imposing donjon of the **Castello di Vertine**, a well-preserved slice of the 13th century and one of the most striking sights in all Chianti. To the east of Gaiole stands the ancient fortified village of **Barbischio**, and just 3km south on S408 is the impressive medieval **Castello di Meleto** with its sturdy cylindrical towers still intact. From here the road continues another 4.5km up to the mighty **Castello di Castagnoli**, guarding a fascinating medieval town in a commanding position.

Most majestic of all is the Iron Baron's celebrated isolated **Castello di Brolio** (*open daily 9–12 and 3 to sunset*), some 10km south of Gaiole along SS484, high on its own hill with views for miles around. First mentioned in 1009, when Matilda of Tuscany's father Bonifacio donated it to the monks of the Badia in Florence, it came into the possession of the Ricasoli in 1167. The castle was bombarded for weeks in 1478 by the Aragonese and Sienese, who later had it demolished, so the 'the walls levelled with the earth'. After the war, Florence rebuilt it, and in the mid-19th century Baron Ricasoli converted it into the splendid fortified residence while experimenting on the modern formula for Chianti ; the Barone Ricasoli Wine House, ✆ (0577) 749 710, offers its famous wines, olive oil, and more. At Madonna del Brolio, 10km to the south, you can also visit the Cantine Barone Ricasoli by phoning ahead, ✆ (0577) 311 961. The Fattoria dei Pagliaresi, ✆ (0577) 359 070, is located near Castelnuovo Berardenga, between S. Gusmé and Pianella and offers older wines as well as new, and olive oil. There are **riding stables** 5km east at the Fattoria San Giusto, at Monti, ✆ (0577) 363 011. To the south, **Castelnuovo Berardenga** is an agricultural centre with the remains of a 14th-century castle.

In the Steps of Piero

This is a journey for art-lovers into the heart of Piero della Francesca country. Abutting Umbria, the Valtiberina or upper valley of Old Father Tiber is a serene, hilly land, a patchwork of pasturelands and pine and beech woodlands, where the light seems more luminous than elsewhere in the region. This is especially true on certain cool, clear days, when the land-scape can seem as uncanny as one of the paintings Piero left behind in his native haunts.

Lunch is in a hearty *locanda* just outside Anghiari, the site in 1440 of victory by the Florentines over the Milanese. Leonardo da Vinci chose it as his subject matter in the *Battle of the Frescoes* in Florence's Palazzo Vecchio—one of the Renaissance's greatest unfinished works, though the cartoons left behind by the master were often copied and became one of the inspirations of Florentine Mannerism.

Locanda al Castello di Sorci

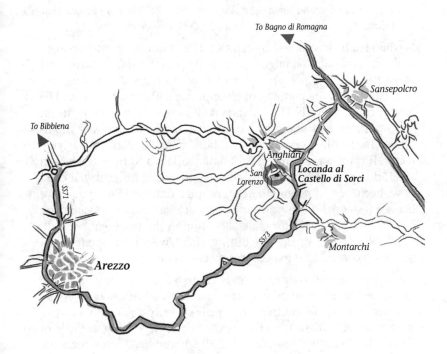

To Bagno di Romagna

Sansepolcro

To Bibbiena

Anghiari

San Lorenzo

Locanda al Castello di Sorci

SS71

SS73

Montarchi

Arezzo

getting there

Head east along the SS73 from Arezzo towards Sansepolcro. After about 30km there's a large advertising hoarding pointing left to the Locanda al Castello di Sorci, followed by a road sign to San Lorenzo and Anghiari. The Locanda is clearly signed again just after the turn.

Locanda al Castello di Sorci

Via San Lorenzo, San Lorenzo, nr Anghiari, ✆ (0575) 789 066. Closed Mon & June. Set meal with unlimited wine L27,000, Mastercard.

Surrounded by woods, overlooking a castle, and with a weather-worn olive press outside, you might imagine the Locanda al Castello di Sorci to be a romantic place where couples talk in hushed tones and the loudest noise is the popping of champagne corks. Nothing could be further from the truth. The Locanda is an earthy, no-nonsense Tuscan insitution, its two floors and numerous blackened-beamed rooms packed in the summer months with holidaying families and partying locals. If there was a canteen for estate workers and their families in the 15th century, when the Castello di Sorci was in its heyday, it can't have been very different to the Locanda today. Unless you have booked (essential if you want one of the few tables in the *loggia*) you have to join the queue for table allocation in the stone-slabbed hall. You'll be asked how many are dining, then given a slip of paper and brusquely commanded to occupy a specific room.

Once you've found your room (easy enough if you know your *sottos*, *sopras*, *destras* and *sinistras*) you sit at an empty table wondering where the menu, water and waitress are, until suddenly a girl with a tray of wine appears, and swiftly circuits the room, depositing a bottle of chilled unlabelled red on each table. She disappears, then repeats the routine with jugs of water, followed by plates of *crostini* and *affettati*. These are not bad at all, slices of crumbly home-baked bread with toppings of tomato, herb butter and chicken liver pâté along with slices of soft, sticky *finocchiona* and hard, chewy peppered *salame*.

All the pasta is home-made, yolk-yellow and springy, served *al dente* on large oval plates so you can help yourself. What you get depends on the day: Tuesday is *tagliolini con fagioli*, Wednesday is *quadrucci con ceci*, Thursday is *gnocchi*, Friday *ribollita*, Saturday *farro* and *risotto con funghi* (in summer, *polenta* in winter), Sunday *polenta* or *risotto con funghi* again depending on the season. Every day you'll also get a plate of *tagliatelle* (you can watch the ladies at work in the kitchen downstairs after lunch). We struck on *gnocchi* day, and despite coming ready-parmesaned they were pretty good—hot, melting and with a fine grainy texture. The *ragù*, made out of leftover cooked lamb, just as canny *mamma* would at home, was pretty tasty too, though it lost some of its charm on a second appearance.

Then come the *secondi*, a platter of grilled chicken and lamb along with a selection of stuffed vegetables. The chicken, a scrawny specimen, was a surprisingly gutsy triumph, full of taste and texture and bearing as much resemblance to a battery bird as Mozart does Muzak. Pudding consisted of a huge slice of crumbly, sugar-frosted lemon sponge and a bottle of *vin santo*, so you can dunk to your heart's content. Coffee is served *in piedi*, downstairs at the bar. After lunch, no one seems anxious to leave. Kids play on the olive press, young couples wander into the woods, and dads with flushed faces snore on shady benches.

Crostini di Fegatini

Serves 6

Here is a recipe for the most typical of Tuscan crostini.

400g/14oz chicken livers
2 tablespoons extra virgin olive oil
2 garlic cloves
6 bay leaves
3 tablespoons dry white wine
about 250ml/8fl oz light chicken stock
tablespoon capers, preferably preserved in salt, rinsed and finely chopped
4 canned anchovy fillets in olive oil, finely chopped
25g/1oz unsalted butter
12 fairly thick slices coarse country bread
salt and pepper

Clean the livers, removing any fat or connective tissue, and slice into fairly large pieces. Heat the olive oil in a frying pan and add the garlic, bay leaves and livers. Season lightly. Stir-fry over a high heat until the mixture starts sticking. Add the wine, scrape the brown bits from the bottom of the pan and cook over a high heat until the wine evaporates. Add a few tablespoons of the stock, then lower the heat and simmer for 5 minutes.

Remove from the heat and discard the bay leaves. Put the liver mixture through a food mill into a small saucepan.

Add the capers, anchovies and butter to the liver mixture and cook gently, stirring constantly, until all the ingredients are blended. Do not let it boil.

Toast the slices of bread in an oven (preheated to 180°C/350°F (gas mark 4) until golden but still soft inside. If you want you can dip them into the remaining stock. Then spread with the liver mixture and serve immediately.

touring around

From Arezzo, it's a pretty 41km drive to Sansepolcro, especially along SS73, which ascends through the **Foce di Scopetone** (with panoramic views back towards the city) then continues another 17km to the short turn-off for **Monterchi**. Dedicated to Hercules in Roman times, Monterchi is a tiny triangle of a medieval town; while strolling its lanes, don't miss the curious underground passageway around the apse of the parish church, dating back to the Middle Ages but of uncertain purpose. Monterchi is most famous, however, for Piero della Francesca's extraordinary fresco which was in the little chapel at the cemetery. The *Madonna del Parto* (1445) is perhaps the first (and last?) portrayal of the Virgin in her ninth month, a mystery revealed by twin angels who pull back the flaps of a tent, empty but for Mary, weary and melancholy, one eyelid drooping, one hand on her hip, the other on her swollen belly, almost painful to see—one of the most psychologically penetrating paintings of the quattrocento. It is now housed in a former primary school, well signposted from all directions. Details of its recent restoration are exhibited with the painting.

Anghiari (pop. 6200), between Monterchi and Sansepolcro, is a fine old town located on a balcony over the Valtiberina. In Anghiari's Renaissance **Palazzo Taglieschi** at Via Mameli 16, the **Museo delle Arti e Tradizioni Popolari dell'Alta Valle del Tevere** has exhibits relating to traditional crafts of the Upper Tiber Valley. Just over 1km to the southwest, there's the pretty Romanesque **Pieve di Sovara**, and on the Sansepolcro road you can still make out the 8th-century Byzantine origins of **Santo Stefano**.

Sansepolcro (pop. 15,500) is the largest town of the Valtiberina, famous for its lace, its pasta (the Buitoni spaghetti works are just outside the city), and for Piero della Francesca. The painter was born here some time between 1410 and 1420, and given his mother's name as his father died before his birth. Although he worked in the Marches, Arezzo and Rome, he spent most of his life in Sansepolcro, painting and writing books on geometry and perspective until he went blind at the age of 60. Sansepolcro was founded around the year 1000, and like Anghiari belonged to the monks of Camaldoli until the 13th century. The historic centre, with its crew-cut towers, has plenty of character, though a bit dusty and plain after several earthquakes and rebuildings. It is enclosed within well-preserved walls, built by the Tarlati and given a Renaissance facelift by Giuliano da Sangallo. **Piazza Torre di Berta** is the centre of town, where on the second Sunday of September crossbow-men from Gubbio come to challenge the home archers in the Palio della Balestra, an ancient rivalry. Along **Via Matteotti** are many of the city's surviving 14th–16th-century palaces, most notably the Palazzo delle Laudi and the 14th-century palace housing the **Museo Civico** (*open daily 9–1.30 and 2.30–7.30, 2.30–6 winter; adm*). Here you can see Piero della Francesca's masterpiece, the *Resurrection*, an intense, almost eerie depiction of the solemnly triumphant Christ stepping out of his tomb surrounded by sleeping soldiers and a sleeping land, more autumnal than springlike. It shares pride of place with two of Piero's early works, the *Misericordia Polyptych*, a gold-background altarpiece dominated by a serene, giant goddess of a Madonna, sheltering under her cloak members of the confraternity (note the black hood on one) who commissioned the picture, and a damaged fresco of San Giuliano. Other works are by his greatest pupil, Luca Signorelli, a *Crucifixion* (with two saints on the back), Pontormo (*Martyrdom of San Quintino*), Santi di Tito, Mannerist Raffaellino del Colle, and the 16th-century Giovanni de' Vecchi, also of Sansepolcro, whose *Presentation of the Virgin* is interesting for its unusual vertical rhythms. You can see a 16th-century scene of Sansepolcro in the *Pilgrimage of the Company of the Crucifix of Loreto*, a relic of the days of the Black Death, as are the wooden panels of Death (one showing a fine strutting skeleton). Downstairs, a room contains sculptural fragments gathered from the town, including a rather mysterious

12th-century frieze of knights from a local palace; upstairs there's a collection of detached frescoes.

Sansepolcro also has a couple of pretty churches: near the museum is the Gothic church of **San Francesco**, with a fine rose window and portal. The **Duomo** on Via Matteotti was built in the 11th century but has been much restored since; among the art inside is a fresco by Bartolomeo della Gatta and a polyptych by Matteo di Giovanni. Another church, **San Lorenzo**, has a *Deposizione* by Rosso Fiorentino.

Gastronomic Time Travel
in San Gimignano

san Gimignano

In the miniaturist landscape of this corner of Tuscany, San Gimignano, Italy's best-preserved medieval city, is an almost fantastic landmark. From Poggibonsi, or from the Volterra road, its medieval towers, some of them over 50m tall, loom over the surrounding hills. Once, almost every city in central Italy looked like this; more than just defensive strongholds in the incessant family feuds, these towers served as status symbols both for the families and the cities themselves, a visible measure of a town's power and prosperity, even if it also betrayed the bitterness of its internal divisions. Originally there were at least 70 towers (in a town barely one-eighth of a square mile in size). Now only 15 remain, though enough, along with San Gimignano's beautiful streets, churches and public buildings, to give the town the impression of having been hermetically sealed in a time capsule from the Middle Ages. Appropriately enough, tucked into an alleyway just off Piazza del Duomo, is a marvellous restaurant which still serves medieval, Renaissance and even Etruscan dishes.

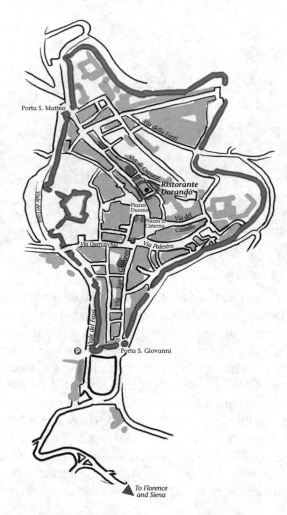

Park outside the town—there's a car park near the Porta di San
Giovanni. From the Porta walk up Via San Giovanni and through
Piazza del Duomo. Just beyond, you'll see a small sign on your
right pointing to Dorandò.

Ristorante Dorandò

*Vicolo dell'Oro 2, (off Piazza Duomo), San Gimignano, © (0577) 941862.
Closed Mon. L65,000, all major credit cards.*

Did you know that Tuscan white beans originated in America? Or that
Catherine de' Medici nearly ate herself to death on chicken liver pâté?
Or that pasta cutters have been discovered in Etruscan tombs? Well, at
Dorandò you can pick up these and other bits of culinary trivia, as you
eat some of the most unusual food in Tuscany. All the recipes here are
based on Etruscan, medieval and Renaissance dishes, many of whose
influences are still felt in the regional cuisine today.

The restaurant, tucked on to a quiet shady back street of San
Gimignano, is housed in a cool, airy 14th-century building, with
vaulted whitewashed ceilings, exposed stone walls and terracotta tiles.
It's a restful, stylish and civilised place, just what you need after
dodging the tour groups flowing up and down nearby Via San Matteo.

The menu describes (in erratic English as well as Italian) the ingredients and history of each dish in detail—often with enough
information for you to be able to repeat the dishes at home. There is
also lots of information about the wines (all grape varieties are listed,
for example), most of which are Tuscan. They start at an extremely
reasonable L9000 for a Vernaccia di San Gimignano. If you fancy
something more unusual, the Castellare di Castellina Spartito
Sauvignon is a good white.

You could start with a rich *cibrèo*, finely diced chicken liver and giblet,
seasoned with ginger and cooked with egg and lemon juice. If you find
it irresistibly moreish, just remember what happened to Catherine de'
Medici. Even more unusual is the salty pungent *sorra marinata con
rucola e dolici*, a marvellous Livornese dish with Etruscan roots. *Sorra* is

Tuscan for white tuna meat, which is traditionally preserved in salt. This is then cut into thin slices and marinated in white wine, vinegar, onions, carrots, garlic, peppercorns, cloves, juniper berries, thyme, bay leaves, parsley and oil.

Several days later it is served with rocket and black eye beans in a sweet, oddly mustardy dressing made by grinding the ingredients of the marinade.

There are equally inspiring *primi*: *pici all'Etrusca*, for example, short, hand-rolled pasta tubes served with a startling mint-leaf *pesto*—definitely one for the recipe book. Another winner is the flavourful *tagliolini con i polpi e funghi*, *tagliolini* served with a sauce made of stewing boiled octopus with onions, garlic, parsley, an anchovy, wild mushrooms and red wine.

Secondi are no disappointment. *Baccalà con patate* is a creamily delicious fasting-day dish, the dried cod soaked so that virtually no trace of salt remains, then mashed with potato, Vernaccia di San Gimignano, herbs and oil, and served as a creamy, comforting mould. *Faraona al ginepro con insalatina* is another hit, the guinea hen highly seasoned with juniper and other spices as it would have been in the Middle Ages when it was necessary to mask the taste and smell of rotting meat. Even though there's no longer any putrefaction to hide, it's a delicious way of cooking game.

Save room for a dessert. Try *lattaiolo*, a delicate coriander-flavoured caramel custard which was popular in the Renaissance; or alternatively one of the ice creams and sherbets which the Medici would serve between the courses of their banquets to aid digestion. If you've still room, round up the meal with a fine *vin santo* and a selection of *cantucci*, and other almondy delicacies.

Pici all'Etrusca

This mint pesto works well with any fine pasta such as linguine. If you want to make your own pasta, try adding a few finely chopped mint leaves to the dough. This is the kind of dish you cook by looking and tasting, so start with roughly equal quantities of pecorino, mint and walnuts, and add more of one or the other to taste. A top-quality olive oil is essential.

a little garlic
walnuts
lots of fresh mint leaves
freshly grated pecorino cheese
extra virgin olive oil (preferably Luccan)
salt and pepper

Chop the garlic, walnuts and mint, then grind all the ingredients with a
pestle and mortar to make a paste—rough or smooth according to taste.
Warm in a bain marie while the pasta is cooking.

touring around

According to legend, the town was originally called Castel della Selva. When the Gothic army of Totila passed through in the 550s, the townsfolk for some reason chose to pray to an obscure saint named Gimignano, a martyred bishop of Modena, for their salvation from what appeared to be a guaranteed sacking. Gimignano came through in style, looming down from the clouds in golden armour to scare away the besiegers.

Even during the Renaissance the town seems to have been a resort for the Florentines; Dante, Machiavelli and Savonarola all spent some time here, and artists like Ghirlandaio and Gozzoli were only too happy to come up for a small commission. Don't let the prospect of crowds keep you from coming. San Gimignano handles them gracefully; its fine art, elegant medieval cityscapes and the verdant rolling countryside right outside its gates make this one of the smaller towns of Tuscany most worth visiting.

Piazza del Duomo and the Museo Civico

On your walk to Dorandò from Porta San Giovanni you will pass the little churches of **San Giovanni**, built by the Knights Templar, and **San Francesco**, with a good Pisan-Romanesque façade, now deconsecrated and converted into a wine shop. Another ancient gate, the Arco dei Bacci, leads into the triangular **Piazza della Cisterna** and the adjacent **Piazza del Duomo**—a superbly beautiful example of asymmetrical medieval town design. Piazza della Cisterna contains the town's well, whence the name, and some of its towers.

On Piazza del Duomo, two stout Gothic public buildings with Guelph crenellations and lofty towers compete with the Collegiata church for your attention. The **Palazzo del Podestà**, with its vaulted loggia, was begun in the 1230s by Emperor Frederick II at the height of Imperial power for his *podestà*. Above it stands the Torre della Rognosa, with a small cupola on top; at 51m it once marked the height limit for private towers—the *podestà* didn't want anyone putting him in the shade. Later, when the *comune* was able to wrest effective self-government from the emperors, it built an even taller tower for the **Palazzo del Popolo** (*open Nov–Feb 9.30–1.30, 2.30–4.30, March, Oct 9.30–6, April–Sept 9.30–7.30, closed Mon*) across the piazza; the awesome 54m Torre Grossa was completed about 1300 and the rest of the Palazzo about 20 years later.

Underneath this tower, an archway leads into the charming, thoroughly medieval **Cortile**, or courtyard, with bits of frescoes (one by Il Sodoma) and the painted coats-of-arms of Florentine governors from after 1353. A stairway leads up to the **Museo Civico** (*open same hours as the tower*), with an excellent collection of art from both Florentine and Sienese masters. One of the oldest works is a remarkable painted crucifix by Coppo di Marcovaldo (c.1270) that predates (and some might say surpasses) the similar, more famous crucifixes of Giotto. The museum has two sweet *Madonnas* by Benozzo Gozzoli, a pair of *tondi* by Filippino Lippi portraying the *Annunciation*, and a big, colourful enthroned *Virgin* of Pinturicchio's that looks as if it strayed here from that artist's Piccolomini chapel in Siena. Taddeo di Bartolo contributes a set of paintings with the definitive *Story of San Gimignano*, a saint worthy of having a town named after him judging by these scenes: he is pictured calming the sea, exorcizing a devil who had been inhabiting the daughter of Emperor Jovian, and succumbing to the flesh while saying mass—he has to pee, but when he sneaks out of church a winged devil attacks him; fortunate enough to have a cross on him, Gimignano drives it away without much difficulty.

To the San Gimignanese, the biggest attraction of the museum is the Sala del Consiglio, or Sala di Dante, where the poet spoke in 1299 as an ambassador of Florence, seeking to convince the *comune* to join the Guelph League. The frescoes on its walls include more works by Gozzoli, a glittering company of angels and saints in the Maestà of the Sienese artist Lippo Memmi, and some trecento scenes of hunting and tournaments. After this, contemplate a climb up the **Torre Grosso** (*see above for opening times; adm*)—several hundred steps, but there's a view over San Gimignano and the surrounding countryside that is worth the effort.

The Collegiata

The name Piazza del Duomo is a little misleading: San Gimignano doesn't have a cathedral any more, but a **Collegiata**, begun in the 12th century and enlarged in the 15th. It turns a blank brick façade towards the world, but the interior is a lavish imitation of Siena cathedral, with its tiger-striped arches and vaults painted with a firmament of golden stars. Its walls, however, outshine the larger cathedral with first-class frescoes of the 14th and 15th centuries, mostly by artists from Siena.

In the north aisle are 14th-century Old Testament scenes by Bartolo di Fredi. Note *Noah with the Animals*, and *The Torments of Job* (also how each scene is accompanied by a neat explanation in simple Italian, a fascinating example of the artists, and the Church, coming to terms with a newly literate public). Some of Bartolo's best work is in the lunettes off the north aisle: a medieval cosmography of the *Creation*, scenes of Adam naming the animals and a graphic view of the creation of Eve. New Testament pictures by Barna da Siena (about 1380) cover the south wall; his *Crucifixion* is an exceedingly fine work. On the west wall, over the entrance, is a well-punctured *Saint Sebastian* by Gozzoli and a real surprise, the most perverse *Last Judgement* in Italy. It isn't recorded what moved Taddeo di Bartolo, a most serendipitous painter of rosy Sienese virgins, to this madness. You may think you have seen the damned suffering interesting tortures and indignities before; Italy has plenty of them. This is the first time, however, that delicacy forbids description. It's a little faded, unfortunately. Nearby stand two wooden figures of an *Annunciation* by Jacopo della Quercia.

The Cappella di Santa Fina

A ticket from the Museo Civico will get you into the chapel of **Santa Fina**, off the south aisle, with an introduction to one of the most irritating hagiographies in Christendom (*open April–Sept 9.30–12.30, 3–6, 3–5.30 Oct–March*). Little Fina was going to the well for water, according to the story, when she accepted an orange from a young swain. Upon returning home, her mother told her how wicked she was to take it, whereupon the poor girl became so mortified over her great sin that she lay down on the kitchen table and prayed for forgiveness without ceasing for the next five years. Finally, St Anthony came down to call her soul up into heaven, and the kitchen table and all the towers of San Gimignano burst into bloom with violets. Domenico Ghirlandaio got the commission to paint all this; he pocketed the money and did a splendid job (1475) in the brightest springtime colours. In the last scene, note San Gimignano's famous towers in the background.

Just to the left of the Collegiata, there is a lovely small courtyard where musicians sometimes play on summer weekends. Here, on the wall of the baptistry, you will see another fine fresco by Ghirlandaio, an *Annunciation* that has survived reasonably well for being outside for 500 years. The town's two other museums are here: the **Museo Etrusco** with a small collection of local archaeological finds, and the **Museo d'Arte Sacra**, which, besides the usual ecclesiastical clutter, has some good painted wood statues from the late Middle Ages (*both open April–Sept 9.30–8, Oct–March 9.30–12.30, 2.30–5.30*).

Around the Town

From Piazza del Duomo, it's not too difficult a climb up to the **Rocca**, a somewhat ruined fortress of the 1350s that offers one of the best views of this towered town. Down Via di Castello, in the eastern end of town, the **Oratory of San Lorenzo in Ponte**, now unused, has quattrocento Florentine frescoes and an exhibit of finds from a 16th–18th-century pharmacy that once functioned in the nearby Hospital of Santa Fina. The busiest and finest street of San Gimignano, however, leaves Piazza del Duomo towards the north: **Via San Matteo**, lined with shops and modest Renaissance palaces. It begins by passing the three truncated **Salvucci Towers**, once the fortified compound of one of San Gimignano's most powerful families (the Salvucci were Ghibellines; the towers of their mortal enemies, the Guelph Ardinghelli, are the ones on the west side of Piazza della Cisterna).

The day-trippers do not often venture into the quiet streets on the north side of town, and so usually miss the church of **Sant'Agostino**, famous for a series of frescoes by Gozzoli on the *Life of St Augustine* on the walls behind the high altar. The merriest of all Renaissance painters has a good time with this one; many of the frescoes are faded and damaged, but not the charming panel where the master of grammar comes to drag sullen little Augustine off to school. Another well-preserved scene shows Augustine in Rome, with most of the city's ancient landmarks visible in the background. Gozzoli also contributed the Saint Sebastian on the left aisle. There is a haunting altarpiece, done by Piero Pollaiuolo in 1483 with an anticipatory touch of the El Greco to it, and some good trecento Sienese painting in a chapel off to the right. Across the piazza from Sant'Agostino, the little church of **San Pietro** has more Sienese painting of that era. Via Folgore di San Gimignano leads off to the northeastern corner of the town; the church of **San Jacopo** stands under the town wall, a simple but interesting building left by the Templars.

Around much of San Gimignano, the countryside begins right outside the wall. There are plenty of opportunities for pleasant after-lunch walks in any direction, and a few landmarks to visit along the way: the **Fonti**, arched medieval well-houses much like Siena's, can be seen just outside the Porta dei Fonti, south of San Jacopo. Further from town, the **Pieve di Cellole** is a pretty 12th-century church in a peaceful setting, 4km west from the Porta San Matteo; its harmonious serenity amid the cypresses inspired Puccini's opera *Suor Angelica*. There are several ruined castles and monasteries within a few miles of the town, and every height offers a different view of San Gimignano's remarkable skyline.

Mob Caps, Pinnies and Monks

Not counting the coastal Maremma around Grosseto, the old territories of the Sienese Republic make a complete and coherent landscape, rolling hills mostly given over to serious farming and pastureland. It isn't as garden-like as some other parts of Tuscany, though tidy vineyards and avenues of cypresses are not lacking. Hill towns, ready landmarks, poke above the horizon—Montalcino, Montepulciano, Pienza; at times it seems the whole region is laid out before you, bounded on one side by the hills around Siena, on the other by the cones of Monte Amiata and Radicófani.

The Sienese would never admit it, but the truth is that the best food in the area is to be found outside the town, not within it. A highlight of any gastronomic tour of the area would have to be a visit to Da Miretta in the hamlet of La Pievina, near Asciano, the kind of restaurant Fellini and Dali would have opened if they'd branched out into the catering trade.

the Abbey of Monte Oliveto Maggiore

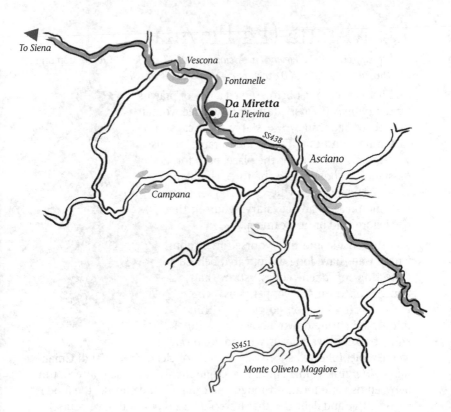

To Siena

Vescona

Fontanelle

Da Miretta
La Pievina

SS438

Asciano

Campana

SS451

Monte Oliveto Maggiore

Appropriately enough, the nearby countryside is pretty Dali-esque, dominated by the *crete* and *biancane*, strange landscapes formed by water erosion.

getting there

Da Miretta is basically all there is to La Pievina, a hamlet about 4km northwest of Asciano on the SS438 which runs towards Siena. As it lies on the roadside (on your right as you approach from Asciano), it is almost impossible to miss: a stone-built inn with two signs, Da Miretta and La Pievina, on its walls.

Da Miretta (La Pievina)

Via Lauretina 9, La Pievina, nr Asciano, © (0577) 718368. Closed Mon and Tues in winter. L65,000 excluding wine, no credit cards.

Could you ever forget being served a tree of prawns? Or ten *antipasti*? Or six desserts? By three women dressed in red and white starry mob caps and matching pinnies? If it's memorable meals you're after, La Pievina is the place, both for its outstanding cooking and the three ebullient, wine-flushed women who cook and serve it. Just one piece of advice: starve yourself the day before, and bring a camera.

You step inside and find yourself in a room whose walls have long disappeared behind a collection of oxen yokes, straw hats, bunches of wheat and copper pans, being greeted as if an honoured guest. Within minutes of sitting down a bowl of peanuts and a basket of warm crusty bread are brought

the prawn tree

to the table, followed shortly by a bottle of clean, fresh Val di Chiana Bianco Vergine Valdi. There is a single menu every day, alternating between fish and meat. Although you can pick and choose, the food is so inventive and delicious that it would be a pity not to give yourself a chance to sample everything.

As soon as you plump for the *degustazione* menu little plates of food begin to arrive in rapid succession. Seafood *crostini* are inspired, the seafood mixed with tomato and a skilful hint of chilli, and served on perfectly cooked toast (crispy on the outside, moist inside). Other dishes might inlude a salad of squid, shrimp and octopus; fresh anchovies; sardines marinated in rosemary and sage (brilliant), smoked mackerel with black pepper and lime; cockles with *ragù* (unexpectedly moreish) and mussels stuffed with breadcrumbs, cheese and tomato.

If you're fortunate, a *zuppa santa* will herald the *primi*, a fish broth enriched with egg and liver whose convalescent powers are much lauded. The first of the pasta dishes was the least original, a single salmon *raviolo* dressed in a rich sauce. The second was *pici* (skinny hand-rolled tubes) served in a fishy, offally, chilli-spiked sauce; the third a seafood *risotto*, the flavours heightened by saffron, flat parsley and chilli.

Next, you'll be offered grilled fish (varieties dependent on the market) and, if you're lucky, that prawn tree. The crustaceans may not taste any different hanging from twigs, but there's no denying the photo opportunities. What's more, with the arrival of the first prawn tree a wave of hilarity begins to unfurl through the room; boundaries between staff, guests (and even English and German tables) dissolve; and the party spirit takes over. The women, now distinctly tipsy, look longingly at the male diners, pressing on them huge home-made *torta di pinoli*, delicate sorbets, ice creams, *cantucci, vin santo* and bottles and bottles of *grappa*.

Tagliatelle alla Marinara

Serves 6

2 tablespoons olive oil
2 cloves garlic, chopped
2 tablespoons chopped flat leaf parsley
pinch of dried chilli flakes
250g/9oz ripe tomatoes, skinned, seeded and chopped
150g/5oz octopus, cleaned and chopped
150g/5oz cuttlefish, cleaned and chopped
150g/5oz fresh prawns, peeled, deveined and chopped
150g/5oz baby squid, cleaned and chopped
a little fish stock (optional)
500g/1lb 2oz tagliatelle
knob of butter
salt and pepper

Heat the oil in a large pan, add the garlic, parsley and chilli flakes and fry for a few minutes. Once the garlic has begun to turn golden add the chopped tomatoes. Cook for 10 minutes, then add the octopus followed by the cuttlefish, prawns and baby squid. Cover and cook for 8–10 minutes. If it gets dry, add a little stock.

Meanwhile cook the tagliatelle in a large pan of boiling salted water, then drain until al dente. Put the fish sauce into a frying pan with the butter. Add the pasta and sauté briefly, then season to taste and serve.

touring around

The countryside around Asciano, 20km southeast of Siena, is dotted with *biancane*, knobbly chalk hills exposed when the soil above erodes away, that often appear in the backgrounds of 14th- and 15th-century Sienese and Florentine paintings. This has always been sheep country, and it suffered much in the changes after Second World War, when many of the men went off to look for work in the cities. Today, immigrants from Sardinia make up a sizeable minority of the population, born shepherds who are trying to get the business back on its feet.

From Siena the SS326 heads east, passing the village of **Monteaperti**, where the Sienese won their famous victory over Florence in 1260, and **Rapolano Terme** (27km), a small spa that retains some of its medieval walls. Besides the hot springs there is a surplus of natural gas in the area, some of it pumped out from wells, and some just leaking out of the ground—don't drop any matches.

If you've made an early start, you should have time to see **Asciano** before lunch. It has walls built by the Sienese in 1351, and a good collection of Sienese art in the **Museo d'Arte Sacra**, next to the Romanesque church of the Collegiata (*open by appointment only,* ✆ *718 207*). From Etruscan necropolises in the area, finds have been assembled in the church of San Bernardino, a modest **Museo Archeologico** (*open daily exc Mon 10–12.30; also 4.30–6.30 June–Sept; adm*). In a house at Via del Canto 11, there are some recently discovered Roman mosaics; ask at the pharmacy on Corso Matteotti to visit. Leaving Asciano on the SS438 towards Siena, you'll come to Da Miretta after about 4km.

After lunch, head back to Asciano, and take the SS451 south to the abbey of **Monte Oliveto Maggiore** and, no less fascinating, the country of the *crete*. In the broken, jumbled hills austere green meadows alternate with ragged gullies and bare white cliffs, uncanny monuments to the power of erosion. At the centre of these *crete*, in the bleakest and most barren part, there is a huge grove of tall, black cypresses around Monte Oliveto Maggiore (*open daily 9.15–12, 3.15–5.45 summer, 3.15–5 winter*). Some of the great gentlemen of Siena's merchant élite founded this monastery, including Giovanni Tolomei and Ambrogio Piccolomini, both jaded merchants and sincere Christians who retired here in 1313 to escape the fatal sophistication of the medieval city. Their new Olivetan Order was approved by the Pope only six years later.

With such wealthy backers, Monte Oliveto became a sort of élite hermitage for central Tuscany. An ambitious building programme carried on throughout the 1400s made it a complete, though little-known monument of quattrocento architecture and art. In its isolated setting, Monte Oliveto is a marvel of Renaissance clarity and rationality, expressed in simple structures and good Siena brick. The beautiful assymmetrical **gatehouse**, decorated with a della Robbia terracotta, makes a fitting introduction to the complex. Inside, the well-proportioned brick **Abbey Church** (finished in 1417) has an exceptional set of wooden intarsia choir-stalls by the master of the genre, Fra Giovanni da Verona, among the best work of this kind in all Italy.

The monastery's greatest treasure, however, is the **Great Cloister**, embellished with 36 frescoes of scenes from the life of St Benedict (whose original rule Tolomei and the Olivetans were trying to restore). The first nine of these are by Luca Signorelli, with formidable ladies and bulky, white-robed monks in the artist's distinctive balloonish forms and sparing use of colour. All the rest are the work of Il Sodoma (1505–8)—some of his best painting, ethereal scenes of Pre-Raphaelite ladies and mandarin monks, with blue and purple backgrounds of ideal landscapes and cities. If you are of that persuasion, popular enough a century ago, that it was with Raphael and Michelangelo that the Renaissance started to go wrong, you owe a visit here. Il Sodoma, not a Florentine or really even a Sienese (he was from Vercelli in the north), wrote the last word of the mainstream tendency of Florentine painting before the excesses of Mannerism. Mr Sodomite himself appears in the scene 'Come Benedetto risaldò lo capistero che era rotta' (How Benedict repaired the broken sieve); he's the dissipated fellow on the left with the white gloves. Look carefully—not only did Sodoma paint himself in, but also his pet badgers, of which he was very fond. The badgers and others of Sodoma's many pets appear in various other frescoes as well.

Unlike so many great Tuscan art shrines, Monte Oliveto, isolated here in the Sienese hills, retains something of its original aloof dignity. Although Napoleon himself suppressed the monastery in 1810, a group of talented brothers still works here, specializing in the restoration of old books.

In the *crete* around Monte Oliveto, the village of **San Giovanni d'Asso** (8km southeast) is built around a Sienese fortress; the church of **San Pietro in Villore** is from the 12th century, with an ambitious, unusual façade. From here a byroad east leads to **Montisi** (7km) and **Trequanda** (12km), two other fine little villages, seldom visited; the latter has a 13th-century castle and another Romanesque church.

An Amorous Retreat

The flat Valdichiana south of Arezzo is the largest, broadest valley in the Apennines, rimmed by surrounding hills and old towns like a walled garden, and famous throughout Italy for its cows. Known as the Chianina, after the valley, and descendants of the primal herds whose fossils were discovered in the vicinity, the cows now provide Tuscany with its prized *bistecca alla fiorentina*. Unusually, the meat is lean, tender and packed with flavour. Consquently there is no need to marinate it: the huge steaks are simply grilled over charcoal or wood-ash, which have been scattered with a few fresh herbs.

But there is more to the Valdichiana than *bistecca alla fiorentina* on the hoof. On both sides of the valley are some of the most beautiful villages in this part of Tuscany, notably Monte San Savino and Lucignano, to say nothing of one of the region's most romantic restaurants, the aptly named Locanda dell'Amorosa, a couple of kilometres south of Sinalunga.

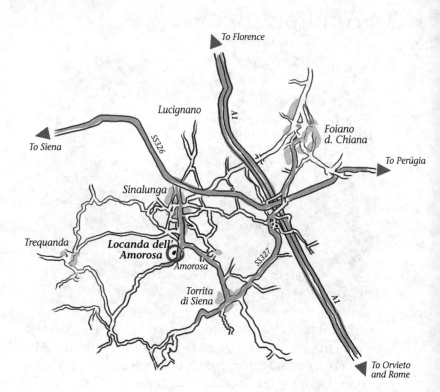

To Florence

Lucignano

A1

*Foiano
d. Chiana*

To Siena

SS326

To Perúgia

Sinalunga

**Locanda dell'
Amorosa**

Trequanda

Amorosa

SS327

*Torrita
di Siena*

A1

*To Orvieto
and Rome*

getting there

This is a nice easy place to find. Simply head out of Sinalunga on
the road to Torrita di Siena. After about two kilometres you'll see a
yellow sign pointing to the right marked Locanda dell'Amorosa.
Unfortunately the turn-off is only a few yards after the sign, so
you'll probably overshoot. So turn back (the road is fairly quiet)
and turn into the avenue of cypresses which climbs the hill to the
minuscule golden-hued hamlet and restaurant.

Locanda dell'Amorosa

Località Amorosa, Sinalunga, © (0577) 679497. Closed Mon lunch and Tues lunch. L65,000, L95,000 exc wine, all credit cards.

If you are going to splash out on a restaurant, there are few better places to do it in Tuscany than the Locanda dell'Amorosa. The setting is idyllic and the food delicious, but, more than that, the service is for once courteous and responsive, a refreshing change from the sneering pretensions and dense inflexibilty which seem par for the course in many of the region's other upmarket establishments.

Amorosa is a tiny hamlet of golden stone patched with russet brick, which formed the core of a medieval estate. Indeed, in Siena's Museo Civico there's a fresco showing the farm as it was in 1300. The farm still produces its own wine. Architecturally, little has changed, though nowadays the manor house has been converted into a small, exclusive hotel, the stables into a restaurant, while the outbuildings are used as larders. Before or after lunch be sure to stroll through the arcaded courtyard which fronts the manor house, to see the church with its fresco fragments and ghoulish martyrdom.

You can eat either inside, in the splendidly vaulted dining room, or outside on a terrace with medieval-looking canopies, a well used as a wait-station, terracotta pots of hydrangeas and views over sunflower fields to the Sienese hills. Kitchen staff in immaculate whites scurrying to and fro with supplies from the storehouses add a bustling getting-ready-for-the-party touch.

As soon as you've settled down, a basket of home-made breads—thin, crisp, herby *croccante*, *focaccia* and sage bread—arrives, along with a bowl of curled butter on crushed ice. The estate white wine, light, fresh, honeyed and perfumed, is kept cool in a copper bucket of ice with lions' head handles.

The menu changes with the seasons, and, sensibly, there are two fixed menus, one (3-course) at L65,000, the other (7-course) at L95,000. However, if you pick and choose, with one person having, say, an *antipasto* and *secondo*, and the other a soup or *primi* and a salad, they may, when not too busy, offer to let you share all the courses.

In season try the salad of creamy raw *porcini*, crumbly parmesan and peppery rocket, the *insalata di alici e razza con olive nere e pomodoro fresco* (fresh anchovy and skate salad with black olives and tomato) or the tarragon-spiked *bavarese di pomodoro con tagliatelle di legumi all'olio e limone* (tomato bavarois with ribbons of raw vegetables).

Even though no attempt is made to give them a nouvelle workover, the traditional soups are not a strong point. The *ribollita*, though dutifully hearty, is too cabbagey for comfort, and though it improves immeasurably when liberally dressed with a luscious olive oil, it nevertheless tends to stick in the throat when you realise you are paying L20,000 for the experience. Better to try one of the more inspired *primi*, like the delicate *risotto ai fiori di zucca e zucchine*, or the pungent *gnocchi di funghi porcini in salsa tartufata*.

There is a good range of *secondi*, divided into fish, grills and *altre carni* (other meats). Most original of the fish dishes is the *scottata di pesci*, a selection of marvellously fresh, barely cooked fish dressed with onion, herbs, oil and lemon. Other fish are more conventionally cooked, partnered with, say, *funghi porcini* or a medley of peppers, aubergines and tomatoes. Star billing on the grill menu goes to the *bistecca di vitellone Chianino 'fiorentina'* (served to a minimum of two), while the choice of more complex meat dishes includes a delicious *petto di faraona ripieno con fichi* (guinea-fowl breast stuffed with figs). Bean-lovers should not miss the perfectly cooked *cannellini* beans which you dress yourself with olive oil.

Desserts do not feature prominently, but there's an excellent selection of cheeses: including fresh, semi-ripe and mature *pecorino*, and goat's cheese with black pepper or herbs.

Risotto ai Fiori di Zucca

Serves 4

1 litre/1¾ pints white meat stock
2 tablespoons finely chopped onion
100g/4oz unsalted butter
250g/9oz arborio rice
1 glass white wine
40 courgette flowers
400g/14oz courgettes, cut into thin strips
100g/4oz parmesan cheese, freshly grated
salt and pepper

Pour the stock into a pan and bring to the boil. Keep it at a simmer while you make the risotto. In a heavy-baked pan fry the onions in half the butter until soft but not coloured. Add the rice and fry gently until slightly translucent. Stir in the white wine, courgette flowers and courgettes and cook over a moderate heat for a few minutes. Add a ladleful of stock and stir until all the liquid has been absorbed by the rice. Keep adding the stock in this way, stirring constantly—it should take 20–25 minutes. Season to taste, stir in the remaining butter, add the parmesan and serve immediately.

touring around

Monte San Savino, on the west side of the Valdichiana valley, was the birthplace of Andrea Contucci, better known as Andrea Sansovino (1460–1529), artistic emissary of Lorenzo de' Medici to Portugal and one of the heralds of the High Renaissance; his Florentine pupil Jacopo adopted his surname and went on to become chief sculptor and architect in Venice in its Golden Age. Monte San Savino, spread out on a low hill on the west rim of the Valdichiana, is an attractive town with a mélange of medieval and fine Renaissance palaces. Andrea Sansovino left his home town an attractive portal on the church of **San Giovanni**, terracottas (along with others by the della Robbias) in the little church of **Santa Chiara**, and the lovely cloister of **Sant'Agostino** (13th-century, with a small rose window by

Guillaume de Marcillat); Antonio da Sangallo the Elder designed the beautiful and harmonious **Loggia dei Mercanti**, with its grey Corinthian capitals (early 1500s, also attributed by some to Sansovino) and the simple, partly rusticated **Palazzo Comunale**, originally the home of the Del Monte family, whose money paid for most of Monte San Savino's Renaissance ornaments. Foremost among the medieval monuments, the **Palazzo Pretorio** was built by the Perugians, while the **city walls** are the work of the Sienese.

On a cypress-clad hill 2km east, **Santa Maria della Vertighe** was built in the 12th century and restored in the 16th; within it holds a 13th-century triptych by Margarito d'Arezzo and, from the next century, works by Lorenzo Monaco. Some 7km to the west there's the pretty hamlet of **Gargonza**, with its mighty tower dominating a tight cluster of houses on a wart of a hill, the whole of which is now a hotel. Best of all, perhaps, is cheerful little **Lucignano**, south of Monte San Savino, unique in the annals of Italian hill towns for its street plan—it will literally run you round in circles: Lucignano is laid out in four concentric ellipses, like a kind of maze, with four picturesque little *piazze* in the centre. One *piazza* is dominated by the **Collegiata** with a theatrical circular stair, another by the 14th-century **Palazzo Comunale**, now the **Museo Civico**, containing a good collection of 13th–15th-century Sienese works, a *Madonna* by Signorelli, and, most famously, a 14th-century masterpiece of Aretine goldsmiths, the delicate reliquary Albero di Lucignano. There are more good Sienese paintings in the little tiger-striped church of **San Francesco**. Outside the centre there's a 16th-century **Medici fortress**, and the Madonna delle Querce, a Renaissance temple sometimes attributed to Vasari, with a fine Doric interior.

South of Lucignano you hit the main Siena-Cortona-Umbria road (SS326) and to the east, **Sinalunga**. There is little to detain you in this light industrial centre, but he main square is named after Garibaldi, to commemorate his arrest here in 1867, on the orders of king Vittorio Emanuele, who was afraid his volunteers were about to attack Rome. **Torrita di Siena**, 6km southwest of the junction with the A1 from Florence to Rome, takes its name from the tall towers of its old walls, some of which remain.

Bean Soup and Brunello

Montalcino is an august walled village, beautifully situated on a hill inhabited since Etruscan times, swathed in vineyards and olive groves.

fortezza. Montalcino

Every year at the Palio in Siena, there is a procession of representatives from all the towns that were once part of the Republic. The honour of leading the parade belongs to Montalcino, for its loyalty and for the great service it rendered in 1555 after the fall of Siena. During the siege, a band of diehard republicans escaped from Siena to the nearly impregnable fortress of Montalcino, where they and the local populace established the 'Republic of Siena at Montalcino', holding out against the Medici until 1559. Today, Montalcino tries hard to be up-to-date (signs on the outskirts proclaim it a *'comune* of Europe' and a 'de-nuclearized zone'); in reality it's a friendly, resolutely sleepy town where people often forget to wind the clocks.

It's a fine choice for a lazy day, for you can while away the hours wandering its streets, drinking in views of the serene countryside below, and browsing in wine shops. For the village's main claim to fame is liquid—a dark, pungent red wine called Brunello di Montalcino that holds a proud place among Italy's finest wines. There are few better accompaniments for the wine than the bean soup and wild boar stew created by the unassuming Trattoria Sciame.

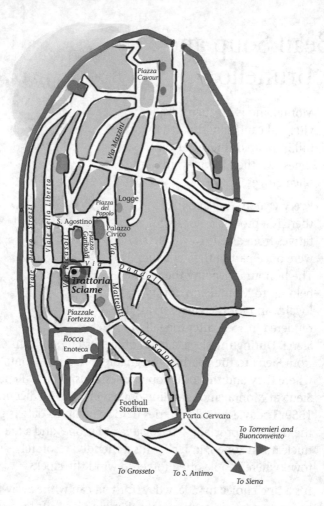

getting there

As you approach Montalcino, follow the signs to the car park at the Rocca. The restaurant lies at the foot of Via Ricasoli, which runs down from the Rocca to the main street, Via Dondoli. Trattoria Sciame lies on the junction of the two.

Trattoria Sciame

Via Ricasoli 9, ✆ (0577) 848017. Closed Mon. L30,000, no credit cards.

Sciame is a mellow family-run *trattoria* in the heart of Montalcino, where you can eat excellent traditional food, including what is probably the best bean soup in Tuscany. It was founded back in the 50s, and although it has recently been given a facelift—pristine white walls and stained pine—it has lost none of its atmosphere, quality or popularity. In fact it is so popular with locals that if you haven't booked you'll probably have to wait. If you arrive and there isn't a table, just ask what time to come back. Then you can either go for a wander or wait in the tiny bar adjoining the restaurant, nibbling peanuts and sipping an aperitif alongside old locals and tourists who have popped in for a freshly cut *prosciutto, salame* or *pecorino* sandwich.

Service is friendly and relaxed—with plenty of help on offer if you need it to select one of the Rosso and Brunello di Montalcinos on the menu. There are some refreshing whites as well if you think a heavy complex red is too much for lunch. With your wine and water comes a basket of fresh crusty bread.

The *antipasti* might be simple and straightforward, but they are excellent: go for the *affettato misto*, a marvellously flavourful selection of locally cured meats and salamis; or the *antipastone*, where the *affettati* come with a *bruschetta* heaped high with cubed tomato. Choosing what is to follow should be easy, given the splendours of the *zuppa di fagioli*, but pasta-lovers may be seduced by the home-made *gnocchi di patate* (served with ragù, mushrooms or—decadently delicious, this— gorgonzola). Alternatively, there's *maccheroni con sugo di cinghiale*, the rich home-made egg pasta bathed in a tangy wild boar sauce. To solve the problem you could always have two *primi*, for that bean soup should not be missed. A rich, flavoursome mingling of long, slowly cooked meat stock, wine, beans and vegetables, it is served with a small red onion on the side, to be slivered on top, a flask of scrumptious olive oil, and, if you need it, grated parmesan.

The *secondi* are superb as well. Sometimes there's *scottiglia*, a mixture of chicken, pork and rabbit or occasionally *cinghiale* (wild boar) braised in an aromatic, piquant sauce and served on slices of toasted bread. Another delicious choice is *arista di maiale al forno*, a tasty roast of locally raised pork. More unexpected is the excellent *baccalà*, firm, flaky and delicate salt cod cooked in a rich tomato sauce.

The *contorni* are fitting tablemates—try a plate of perfectly cooked white beans drizzled with olive oil, or a mixture of potatoes, carrots and yellow pepper ovenbaked to a sweet, soft and melting perfection.

As for pudding, make room for a glass of *moscadello* or *vin santo* with plate of *cantucci* and *ossi di morto*. The latter are a Montalcino speciality, light, dry biscuits made of sugar, egg white and almonds which, as the name suggests, are as brittle as the bones of the dead.

Zuppa di Fagioli

This is a recipe adapted to northern climes where ingredients are less good.

Serves 4

2 tablespoons olive oil

½ teaspoon chilli powder

2 red onions, chopped

2–3 carrots, chopped

1 stick celery (and leaves if they are good), chopped

handful of parsley, chopped

2 (or more) garlic cloves, chopped

glass of dry red wine

225g/8oz cooked borlotti/cannellini beans (or a 400g/14oz tin of beans)

300ml/1/2 pint puréed fresh tomatoes (or tomato passata, or a 400g/14oz tin of tomatoes)

600ml/1 pint good meat stock (game is delicious, beef, veal or chicken are pretty good) or water

handful of spinach, chard or other green leafy vegetable (optional)

salt and pepper

To serve:

olive oil

basil leaves

freshly grated Parmesan cheese

toasted ciabatta bread

1 small red onion

Heat the olive oil in a pan, add the chilli, onions, carrots, celery and parsley and sauté until the vegetables are beginning to get soft. Add the garlic and cook a few minutes longer, then stir in the wine and cook briskly until almost completely evaporated. All in all, you'll probably need to cook the vegetables for around half an hour.

Purée a third of the beans in a liquidizer and add to the pan along with the tomato pulp. Stir, then add the rest of the beans and the stock or water. Cook for another 45 minutes or so, until all the flavours have melded. About 5 minutes before you are ready to eat, place the spinach or other leaves on top of the soup, put on the lid, and turn off the heat. The leaves will wilt in the steam, and should be stirred into the soup before serving.

Serve topped with a drizzle of olive oil and freshly torn basil leaves, with Parmesan, toasted ciabatta, and the red onion on the side to shave on to the soup.

touring around

Start at the eastern end of Montalcino, where you can park outside the impressive 14th-century **Rocca** (*open daily exc Mon 9–1 and 2–8, winter 4–6; adm*), the centre of the fortifications that kept the Spaniards and Florentines at bay. This citadel means a lot to Italian patriots; it was the last stronghold not only of the Sienese, but symbolically of all the medieval freedoms of the Italian cities, blotted out in the bloody, reactionary 1500s. Near the entrance is a plaque with a little poem from the 'Piedmontese Volunteers of Liberty', extolling Montalcino's bravery in 'refusing the Medici thief'. Now a city park, with views that on a clear day stretch over half the province, the Rocca itself contains the last battle standard of the Sienese republic and the knowledgeable and well-stocked Enoteca Drogheria Franci where you can become better acquainted with Montalcino's venerable Brunello and other local wines such as Moscadello and Rosso di Montalcino.

If you're in the mood to eat right away, nip down Via Ricasoli (with Trattoria Sciame at the bottom), past a shop selling a ferocious assortment of reproduction suits of armour and instruments of torture and copper pans. Don't miss, however, a little shop called Apicoltura Ciacci, wholly devoted to honey and bee products.

After lunch you could head back up to the Rocca and follow the **town walls** on the north side, passing through neighbourhoods largely made up of orchards and gardens—Montalcino isn't nearly as busy a place as it was in the 1400s. The **cathedral**, on Via Spagni, was mostly rebuilt in the 1700s. Follow that street past the Baroque church of the **Madonna del Soccorso**, and you come to the **city park**, the 'Balcony of Tuscany', with views over Siena and beyond.

From the church little Viale Roma leads into Piazza Cavour and one of Montalcino's modest museums: the small **Archaeology Museum**, set in a former hospital pharmacy with detached frescoes by a student of Il Sodoma (*see* pp.125–6.). Via Mazzini leads west to the Piazza del Popolo, and the attractive **Palazzo Comunale**, begun in the late 13th century, with a slender tower that apes the Torre di Mangia in Siena. Nearby, **Sant'Agostino** is a simple Sienese church, preserving some original frescoes from the 1300s. The **Diocesan and Civic Museum** around the corner (*open daily exc Mon, summer 9.30–1, 3.30–7pm, winter 10–1, 3–5; adm; reopening after renovations in summer 1996; reduced price combined ticket for the museum and the Rocca is available*) has a collection of Sienese painting and polychromed wood statues, including some of the earliest successes of Sienese art, an illuminated Bible and painted crucifix, both from the 12th century. Besides some minor works of the 14–15th-century Sienese masters, there is a collection of locally produced majolica from the same period.

South of Montalcino, a few of the vineyards that produce the famous Brunello di Montalcino are on the road south for Sant'Antimo. Two of them welcome visitors: the Azienda Agricola Greppo, and the Cantine dei Barbi (© 848087 and 848277 respectively; ring first if you plan to visit). **Sant'Antimo** itself, about 10km south of Montalcino, is worth the detour. One of the finest Romanesque churches in Tuscany, it originally formed part of a 9th-century Benedictine monastery founded, according to legend, by Charlemagne himself. The present building, begun in 1118, includes parts of the Carolingian works, including the crypt.

This half-ruined complex could easily serve as the set for *The Name of the Rose*. An important monastic community once flourished here; what buildings remain are now used as barns. The church, though, is exquisite, with its elegant tower and rounded apse. Some of the stone inside, on the capitals and elsewhere, is luminous alabaster from Volterra. The sophistication of the architecture is impressive—in particular the Byzantine-style women's gallery, and the ambulatory behind the apse with its radiating chapels.

A Culinary Glossary

The full Italian culinary vocabulary is enormous, and several pocket guides are available that give extensive lists of the many terms and phrases. The following should, though, provide some of the necessary basics.

Useful Words and Phrases

yes/no/maybe	*si/no/forse*
I don't know	*Non lo so*
I don't understand (Italian)	*Non capisco (l'italiano).*
Does someone here speak English?	*C'è qualcuno qui che parli inglese?*
Speak slowly	*Parla lentamente*
Please	*Per favore*
Thank you (very much)	*(Molte) grazie*
You're welcome	*Prego*
Excuse me	*Scusi*
Good morning	*Buongiorno* (formal hello)
Good afternoon/evening	*Buona sera* (also formal hello)
Goodnight	*Buona notte*
Goodbye	*Arrivederla* (formal), *arrivederci, ciao* (informal)
What do you call this in Italian?	*Come si chiama questo in italiano?*
I would like...	*Vorrei...*
That was wonderful	*Era buonissimo*
Where is the bathroom?	*Dov'è il bagno?*
It is too late	*È troppo tardi*
Monday	*lunedì*
Tuesday	*martedì*
Wednesday	*mercoledì*
Thursday	*giovedì*
Friday	*venerdì*
Saturday	*sabato*
Sunday	*domenica*

Italian Menu Vocabulary

Can I book a table (for two) at 1pm?	*Posso prenotare un tavolo (per due) per l'una?*
Lunch	*Pranzo*
Dinner	*Cena*
Excuse me	*Scusi*
What are the specialities of the house?	*Quali sono le specialità della casa?*
Degustazione	Menu where you sample a little of many dishes
The wine list, please	*La carta dei vini, per favore.*
Another bottle of white wine, please	*Un'altra bottiglia di vino bianco, per favore.*
Mineral water (fizzy)	*Un'acqua minerale*
Still	*senza gas*
Fizzy	*con gas*

Antipasti (Hors-d'œuvres)

antipasto misto	mixed antipasto
antipasto misto mare	mixed fish and seafood antipasto
bruschetta	garlic toast
bruschetta con pomodoro	garlic toast with tomatoes
carciofi (sott'olio)	artichokes (in oil)
crostini Toscani	chicken liver paté on toast
finocchiona	a rather soft salami flavoured with fennel seeds
frutti di mare	seafood
panzanella	Tuscan bread, tomato and garlic salad
peperonata	stewed peppers, onions and tomatoes
prosciutto (con melone/fichi)	cured ham (with melon/figs)
salsiccia	dry sausage

Primi: Minestre e Pasta (First Courses: Soups & Pasta)

agnolotti	ravioli with meat
caciucco	spiced fish soup

cannelloni	meat and cheese rolled in pasta tubes
cappelletti	small ravioli, often in broth
crespelle	crêpes
farfalle	butterfly-shaped pasta
fettuccine	long strips of pasta
frittata	omelette
gnocchi	little potato dumplings
lasagne	sheets of pasta baked with meat and cheese sauce
minestra di verdura	thick vegetable soup
minestrone	soup with meat, vegetables, and pasta
orecchiette	ear-shaped pasta, usually served with turnip greens
pappa al pomodoro	Tuscan bread and tomato soup
pappardelle alla lepre	flat pasta ribbons with hare sauce
passato	a liquidised, sieved or *moulie*d soup
pasta e fagioli	soup with beans, bacon, and tomatoes
penne all'arrabbiata	quill shaped pasta in hot spicy tomato sauce
polenta	cake or pudding of corn semolina, prepared with meat or tomato sauce
ribollita	Thick soup of vegetables, and beans, traditionally made by reheating yesterday's minestrone with bread and cabbage
risotto (alla milanese)	Italian rice (with saffron, chicken stock and wine)
spaghetti all'amatriciana	with spicy sauce of bacon, tomatoes, onions, and hot pepper
spaghetti alla bolognese	with ground meat, ham, mushrooms, etc.
spaghetti alla carbonara	with bacon, eggs, and black pepper
spaghetti al pomodoro	with tomato sauce

spaghetti al sugo/ragù	with meat sauce
spaghetti alle vongole	with clam sauce
stracciatella	broth with eggs and cheese
tagliatelle	flat egg noodles
tagliolini	thinner tagliatelle
tordelli	a Luccan speciality: big stuffed pasta
tortellini al pomodoro/panna/in brodo	pasta caps filled with meat and cheese, served with tomato sauce/cream, or in broth
tortelloni	large stuffed pasta
vermicelli	very thin spaghetti
zuppa di fagioli	bean soup
zuppa di farro	spelt soup
zuppa santa	fish broth enriched with egg and liver

Secondi: Carne (Second Courses: Meat)

abbacchio	milk-fed lamb
agnello	lamb
anatra	duck
animelle	sweetbreads
arista	pork loin
arrosto misto	mixed roast meats
bistecca alla fiorentina	huge T-bone beef steak which should be from the Chianina valley, best grilled over an open fire
bocconcini	veal mixed with ham and cheese and fried
braciola	chop
brasato di manzo	braised meat with vegetables
bresaola	dried cured beef
capretto	kid
capriolo	roe deer
carne di castrato/suino	mutton/pork
carpaccio	thin slices of raw beef
cervello	brains
cervo	venison
cinghiale	boar

coniglio	rabbit
cotoletta (alla milanese)	veal cutlet (fried in breadcrumbs)
fagiano	pheasant
faraona	guinea fowl
involtini	rolled slices of veal with filling
inzimino	stew of squid and greens
lepre	hare
lombo di maiale	pork loin
maiale	pork
manzo	beef
ossobuco	braised veal knuckle with herbs
pancetta	streaky bacon
pernìce	partridge
petto di pollo	boned chicken breast
piccione	pigeon
pollo	chicken
polpette	meatballs
quaglia	quail
rana	frog
rognoni	kidneys
saltimbocca	veal scallop with prosciutto and sage, cooked in wine and butter
scaloppine	thin slices of veal sautéed in butter
spezzatino	pieces of beef or veal, usually stewed
spiedino	meat on a skewer or stick
stufato	beef braised in white wine with vegetables
tacchino	turkey
trippa	tripe
uccelletti	small birds usually on a skewer
vitello	veal

Secondi: Pesce (Second Courses: Fish)

acciughe or *alici*	anchovies
anguilla	eel
aragosta	lobster
aringa	herring

baccalà	dried cod
bonito	small tuna
branzino	sea bass
calamari	squid
cappe sante	scallops
cefalo	grey mullet
coda di rospo	angler fish
cozze	mussels
datteri di mare	razor (or date) mussels
dentice	dentex (perch-like fish)
dorato	gilt head
fritto misto	mixed fish fry, with squid and shrimps
gamberetto	shrimp
gamberi (di fiume)	prawns (crayfish)
granchio	crab
insalata di mare	seafood salad
lamprèda	lamprey
merluzzo	cod
nasello	hake
orata	bream
ostriche	oysters
pescespada	swordfish
polpo	octopus
pesce azzuro	various types of small fish
pesce San Pietro	John Dory
rombo	turbot
sarde	sardines
seppie	cuttlefish
sgombro	mackerel
sogliola	sole
squadro	monkfish
storione	sturgeon
tonno	tuna
triglia	red mullet (rouget)
trota	trout
trota salmonata	salmon trout
vongole	small clams
zuppa di pesce	mixed fish in sauce or stew

Contorni (Side Dishes, Vegetables)

asparagi	asparagus
carciofi	artichokes
cardi	cardoons
carote	carrots
cavolfiore	cauliflower
cavolo	cabbage
cavolo nero	a very dark-leafed cabbage
ceci	chickpeas
cetriolo	cucumber
cime di rapa	turnip tops
cipolla	onion
fagioli	white beans
fagiolini	French (green) beans
fave	fava beans
finocchio	fennel
fiori di zucca	courgette flowers
funghi (porcini)	mushrooms (ceps)
insalata (mista, verde)	salad (mixed, green)
lattuga	lettuce
lenticchie	lentils
melanzana	aubergine/eggplant
ortiche	nettles
patate	potatoes
peperoni	sweet peppers
peperonata	stewed peppers, onions and tomatoes etc
piselli (al prosciutto)	peas (with ham)
pomodoro	tomato
porri	leeks
radicchio	red chicory
radice	radish
rapa	turnip
sedano	celery
spinaci	spinach
verdure	greens
zucca	pumpkin
zucchine	zucchini (courgettes)

Formaggio (Cheese)

bel paese	a soft white cow's cheese
cacio/caciocavallo	pale yellow, often sharp cheese
fontina	rich cow's milk cheese
groviera	gruyere
gorgonzola	soft blue cheese
parmigiano	Parmesan cheese
pecorino	sheep's cheese
provolone	sharp, tangy cheese; *dolce* is more mild
ricotta	fresh, soft, low fat, sheep or cows milk cheese

Frutta (Fruit, Nuts)

albicocche	apricots
ananas	pineapple
arance	oranges
banane	bananas
cachi	persimmons
ciliegie	cherries
cocomero	watermelon
dattero	date
fichi	figs
fragole (con panna)	strawberries (with cream)
frutta di stagione	fruit in season
lamponi	raspberries
macedonia di frutta	fruit salad
mandarino	tangerine
melagrana	pomegranate
mele	apples
melone	melon
mirtilli	bilberries
more	blackberries
nespola	medlar fruit
nocciole	hazelnuts
noci	walnuts
pera	pear
pesca	peach
pesca noce	nectarine

pinoli	pine nuts
pompelmo	grapefruit
prugna/susina	plum
uva	grapes

Dolci (Desserts)

amaretti	macaroons
cantucci con vin santo	hard almond biscuits, best dipped in vin santo, dessert wine
castagnaccio	cake of chestnut flour and rosemary
coppa gelato	assorted ice cream
crema caramella	caramel-topped custard
crostata	fruit flan
gelato (produzione propria)	ice cream (homemade)
osso di morti	biscuits of egg white, sugar and nuts
panettone	sponge cake with candied fruit and raisins
panforte	dense cake of chocolate, almonds, and preserved fruit
semifreddo	refrigerated cake
sorbetto	sherbet
tiramisù	mascarpone, coffee, chocolate and sponge fingers
torta	tart
torta di castagne	chestnut cream tart
zabaglione	whipped eggs, sugar and Marsala wine, served hot
zuppa inglese	trifle

Bevande (Beverages)

acqua minerale con/senza gas	mineral water with/without fizz
latte	milk
tè	tea
caffè	espresso
macchiato	espresso with a little milk
vino (rosso, bianco, rosato)	wine (red, white, rosé)

Cooking Terms, Miscellaneous

aceto (balsamico)	vinegar (balsamic)	*miele*	honey
affumicato	smoked	*mostarda*	candied mustard sauce
aglio	garlic	*olio*	oil
alla brace	on embers	*pane (tostato)*	bread (toasted)
bicchiere	glass	*panini*	sandwiches
burro	butter	*panna*	fresh cream
cacciagione	game	*pepe*	pepper
conto	bill	*peperoncini*	hot chili peppers
costoletta/cotoletta	chop	*piatto*	plate
coltello	knife	*prezzemolo*	parsley
cotto adagio	braised	*ripieno*	stuffed
cucchaio	spoon	*rosmarino*	rosemary
disossato	boned	*sale*	salt
filetto	fillet	*salmì*	wine marinade
forchetta	fork	*salsa*	sauce
forno	oven	*salvia*	sage
fritto	fried	*senape*	mustard
ghiaccio	ice	*tartufi*	truffles
griglia	grill	*tazza*	cup
limone	lemon	*tavola*	table
magro	lean meat/ or pasta without meat	*tovagliolo*	napkin
		tramezzini	finger sandwiches
mandorle	almonds	*umido*	cooked in sauce
marmellata	jam	*uovo*	egg
menta	mint	*zucchero*	sugar

Recipes